CANINE COGNITIVE SKILLS

KAY ATTWOOD

Thank you to….

All my customers, past and present, who have allowed me to experiment
with their dogs' thinking processes in order to for me to have found a way to use
these exercises in workshops all around the world. Also, a special thank you to the dogs
and handlers who gave up their time to help with the photography for this book.

Thanks also go to my good friends (and customers too),
Anna Laney and Paul Hadlow for their invaluable advice and input.

Thank you also to my husband for allowing me to stay away from home
so many times without complaining, and my dogs for being
super enthusiastic 'guinea pigs' when I have a crazy idea for a new game!

And finally, to Westline Publishers, for their patience
whilst I was writing this book for you and your dogs.

Thank you all from the bottom of my heart.

This book is dedicated to my customers, who have attended my workshops
and allowed me to 'play' and learn about their dogs' thought processes
and problem-solving abilities and antics.
It is has been a very great privilege.

Studio Photography
LAURA HIRONS
Laura Hirons Photography
www.laurahironsphotography.com

First published in 2024 by First Stone Publishing an imprint of
Westline Publishing Limited
The Old Hen House, St Martin's Farm, Zeals, BA12 6NZ, United Kingdom

Copyright 2024 Kay Attwood and Westline Publishing Limited

ISBN 9781910488713

CONTENTS

INTRODUCTION   4
How it all began.

Chapter One: THE DOG'S BRAIN   7
The canine brain; Neural pathways; Cognitive learning (Intrinsic factors; Extrinsic factors); The five cognitive skills (1. Attention; 2. Memory; 3. Logic and reasoning; 4. Auditory and visual processing; 5. Cognitive flexibility); Bringing about behaviour change (Reactive dogs; Frustration tolerance).

Chapter Two: REINFORCEMENT STRATEGIES   21
What does your dog want? The question of punishment; Understanding reinforcers (Primary reinforcers; Secondary reinforcers; Tertiary reinforcers; Working with different reinforcers); The three-way route; Your very own three rewards; Rates of reinforcement.

Chapter Three: HOW TO TEACH COGNITIVE SKILLS   30
Types of learning (The effect of stress); Making choices (Learning to choose): Setting up for success (Keep it short and sweet; Pipe down; Dealing with distractions).

Chapter Four: FOUNDATION SKILLS   40
Working for food; Anchor position; Voluntary eye contact; Four-point action plan (1. Tap; 2. Touch; 3. Push; 4. Look); Show me.

Chapter Five: LET THE GAMES COMENCE!   50
Audi discrimination; Roll and reveal; Find my face; Ignoring visual distractions; Catchy, Catchy monkey; Cover up; Push over; Wait for it! Switching focus.

Chapter Six: INCREASING THE CHALLENGE   62
Find my keys; Tidy up; Press the button; Noughts and crosses; Little and large; Show and tell; Find the toy; Muffin man – take one; Muffin man – take two.

Chapter Seven: MASTER CLASS   80
Keeping watch; Watch, smell, remember; Talking pictures; Count the spots; Colour discrimination; Colour match; Chase the ace; Picture recall; Like for like.

In Conclusion   95

Introduction

Have you ever wondered how intelligent your dog is? Or perhaps, you think your dog is not that intelligent at all? If you think the latter, you are not alone, as I have met many owners over the years, who, at first, thought their dog was quite dim!

Granted, at times dogs appear to do the silliest of things and we can only wonder what on earth is going on in their heads. But, trust me, regardless of age or breed, each and every dog possesses an amazing brain with amazing capabilities. All we need to do is to tap into that brain through games and by teaching skills which will open up behaviour changing opportunities.

Yes, both training and games *can* and *do* have a profound impact on your dog's behaviour. Whether you want to add enrichment, take on training challenges, or change behaviour, this book will show you how to turn your dog into a thinking machine with a brand-new repertoire of tricks and skills. Some of the cognitive skills I teach will be new to you, and some can be added to existing tricks, perhaps giving a layer of finesse. But, more importantly I will introduce you to a whole new way of seeing your dog: how he thinks, how his brain works – and give you the opportunity to show off to your family and friends!

Dogs have lived with humans for thousands of years, but it is only in the last 50 years or so that we have started to realise that they are amazing thinkers and problem-solvers. When I first started my dog training journey in 2006, we did not consider a dog's mental processes. We did not question what he was thinking about, what he could be thinking about, or whether he was thinking at all! We were responding to the behaviour we could see, not the thinking behind it. Now, as we gain more knowledge of domestic dogs – how they learn, and how they have evolved over the years – we are starting to appreciate that they possess brain functions of a superior nature.

How intelligent is your dog?

Observational research has been carried out worldwide to evaluate the dog's mental powers, his thought processing and decision-making, the strategies he adopts, and how he approaches a problem and goes about solving it. Most dog cognition research, conducted in a far more formal environment than my classes and workshops, is strictly observational. In my workshops and classes, we are looking for 'above average' results, rather than 100 per cent accuracy, which would be asking too much of the dog, not to mention the owner! Instead, we involve the dogs in a variety of fun games and problem-solving exercises. We observe how they make decisions and choose strategies, which enables us to learn about their behaviour and cognitive processes.

Once the dog has learned a route to reinforcement, i.e., he is rewarded for behaviour leading to the correct goal, and/or the fastest route to getting reinforcement, accuracy improves a great deal. Interestingly, I have discovered from observing these exercises that it is not just the reward – a tasty food treat – that acts as a reinforcer; the dog is motivated by intrinsic reinforcers, such as enjoyment derived from performing the task itself.

HOW IT ALL BEGAN

My knowledge of the cognitive ability of dogs, and my research, has been reliant on the co-operation of thousands of guardians and their dogs. I have worked closely with these partnerships since 2005, and I am grateful to each and every one of them. Many have learnt how to expand their repertoire far beyond basic obedience, learning successfully as a team. Generally, there are only so many obedience classes you can do before you and your dog are ready for a change, a new challenge, something to get your teeth into and extend your learning. Many of the dogs attending my classes, over the years, had social issues in one form or another, but I still allowed them to attend. I believe that all dogs and guardians should be allowed to spend quality time together and given the opportunity to learn. This was a strategy that paid off spectacularly. It soon became evident that these dogs, with known social issues, were learning to cope in an environment where there were other dogs and people purely because they were using a different part of their brain and, more importantly, they were enjoying themselves!

During these classes I also observed a fundamental shift in the way these dogs behaved towards the other dogs and people in the class who may, previously, have triggered negative responses. Those who were nervous became more confident about the skills they were learning and began to offer lots of behaviours in an effort to solve the various tasks they were given. Those who had previously used aggression as a tool to cope with insecurities no longer felt the need to do so. I believe this is the direct result of a chemical change in the brain, and in the hormones that the dogs were producing, triggered by the exercises and challenges that were being presented to them.

On my training journey, I have benefitted from getting to know a number of distinguished academics and dog experts, some of whom have become close friends. I have also attended many conferences, watched hundreds of dvds and read countless books, all of which have had a huge impact on my education and on-going professional development, and will likely continue to do so. However, yet again, I have to thank my dog and guardian teams for bringing about the biggest change in my training.

I had been teaching advanced classes over a number of years, and my students kept coming back for more! This was great but, obviously they wanted to learn something new. This forced me to think outside of the box, change the format, and present fresh challenges. As my students got better, I had to get better at teaching new things to keep them engaged and stimulated. I needed to think up new games and exercises, which, in turn, stretched me and challenged me to become a better trainer. This heralded the start of my cognitive skills workshops, which focus on acquiring new skills, utilising memory, changing behaviour patterns – and simply having fun!

My aim in this book, is to provide an understanding of how the dog's brain works: how he processes and recalls information, how he makes decisions and how he solves problems. To encourage and develop these skills I have outlined a series of exercises and games, using step-by-step instructions. They cover all levels – from beginner to advanced – and most of the equipment that is used can be found in your own home. Regardless of whether you are training your dog to be a top-class competitor in one of the canine disciplines, or you are simply enjoying spending quality time with your pet dog, brain games will be hugely beneficial.

So do not delay; start turning these pages, fire up your dog's brain, and embark on a training journey that will be fun and enjoyable, and will enhance and enrich the bond between you.

We will explore what cognition is and how it works for your dog. But be warned: once you show your dog how easy it is to think for himself, and to show you what he wants and what he is thinking, you will open up a whole new world which can become highly addictive for you both!

Chapter One
UNDERSTANDING THE CONCEPT

As a professional dog trainer of many years standing, I have yet to meet a stupid dog! As a species, dogs have relied on their brains in order to survive and to adapt, evolving from their wolf ancestors to become the highly successful domesticated dog we know today. They have learnt what they want and need in order to survive, and they have also learnt what to avoid in order to stay safe. These are self-taught lessons, using knowledge accrued from experience and then passing it on to others within their family group or social group, over years of evolution.

So we know that dogs can process information, make decisions and problem-solve. They have the cognitive skills, but for many individuals these remain dormant. The domesticated dog no longer needs to use his wits in order to survive. We provide food, shelter and safety, so surely our dogs are perfectly happy jogging along, relying on us to make all the decisions.

Obviously we cannot quantify what makes our dogs happy or content, but imagine what it would be like living in a black-and-white world, with little or no stimulation, and no opportunity for growth and development. It would be akin to sleepwalking through life rather than living it.

So let us start by looking at the benefits that can be derived from developing a dog's cognitive skills:

On a simple level, it will:
- Give young dogs a chance to use their developing brains.
- Provide mental stimulation for dogs of all ages to keep their minds active.
- Allow opportunities for enrichment.
- Provide a low impact activity for older dogs, or those recovering from illness or surgery.
- Allow dogs and guardians to spend quality time together, thus enhancing the bond between them.

On a deeper level, it can be the means of:
- Improving cognitive abilities – including memory, decision-making and problem solving – which can be highly beneficial in sporting/competitive situations.
- Acquiring focus and ignoring distractions – useful in everyday life, and key to success in challenging competition environments.
- Decreasing anxieties and restoring peace of mind.
- Keeping dementia at bay.
- Changing behaviour.

To understand why using and improving cognitive skills has such far-reaching effects, we need to understand the nature of cognition. In simple terms this means:

The mental action or process of acquiring knowledge **(dog training)** *and understanding* **(learning the exercises taught in a class or at home)** *through thought* **(decision-making and learning)**, *experience and the senses* **(how the dog feels as a result of the training)**.

In recent times, 'cognition' has become something of a buzz word in the dog training industry. This is no bad thing, as deepening our knowledge regarding brain function can only improve our training and make it more effective. However, we need to strive for a clear understanding rather than getting carried away by the hype!

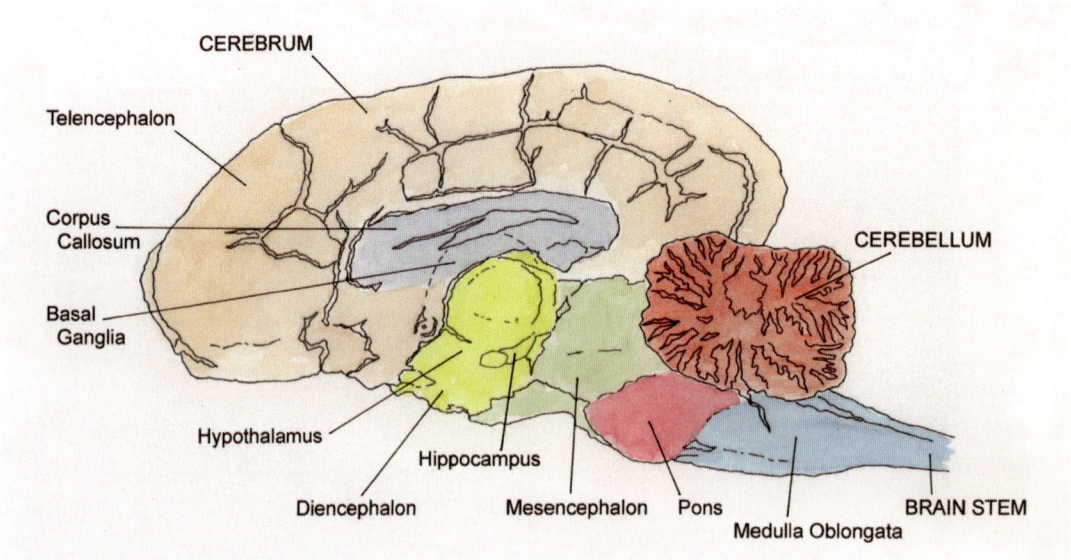

The canine brain.

THE CANINE BRAIN

To find out more about cognition, and teaching cognitive skills, let us take a look at how the dog's brain functions.

The brain is divided into three main sections:

1. **BRAIN STEM:** This connects the brain to the spinal cord and sends messages to the brain to control basic life functions, such as heartbeat, breathing, balance, coordination, and reflexes.
2. **CEREBRUM:** The centre of conscious decision-making. It is the largest part of the brain and is made up of two cerebral hemispheres: an outer and inner section (grey and white matter).
3. **CEREBELLUM:** Involved in movement and motor control.

There are further sub-divisions:

TELENCEPHALON
This is where sensory experiences are interpreted and where thought processing is instigated. It occupies a larger space than in the human brain, so the ears, nose, and eyes are exceptionally sensitive.
Responsible for:
- Personality.
- Social behaviour.

DIENCEPHALON
This relays sensory information between the brain regions and controls autonomic functions of the peripheral nervous system. It also connects structures of internal organs with the nervous system. The diencephalon is highly advanced in dogs, evidenced by fast reflexes, agility, excellent hearing, etc.
Responsible for:
- Chewing.
- Breathing.
- Regulating digestion.
- Heartbeat.
- Swallowing.

MESENCEPHALON
Also referred to as the mid-brain, this important part of the brain is responsible for motor control and function, and

transmitting information to other brain regions.

Responsible for:
- Finer muscular skills/motor control.
- Transmission of vision and hearing.
- Regulation of temperature.
- Reward centre – drives behaviour in response to things that are pleasurable/rewarding.

CORPUS CALLOSUM

This is a bundle of nerve cells that connects the left and right spheres of the brain. The size is dependent on breed, along with speed of function.

Responsible for:
- Communication between the telencephalon and diencephalon.

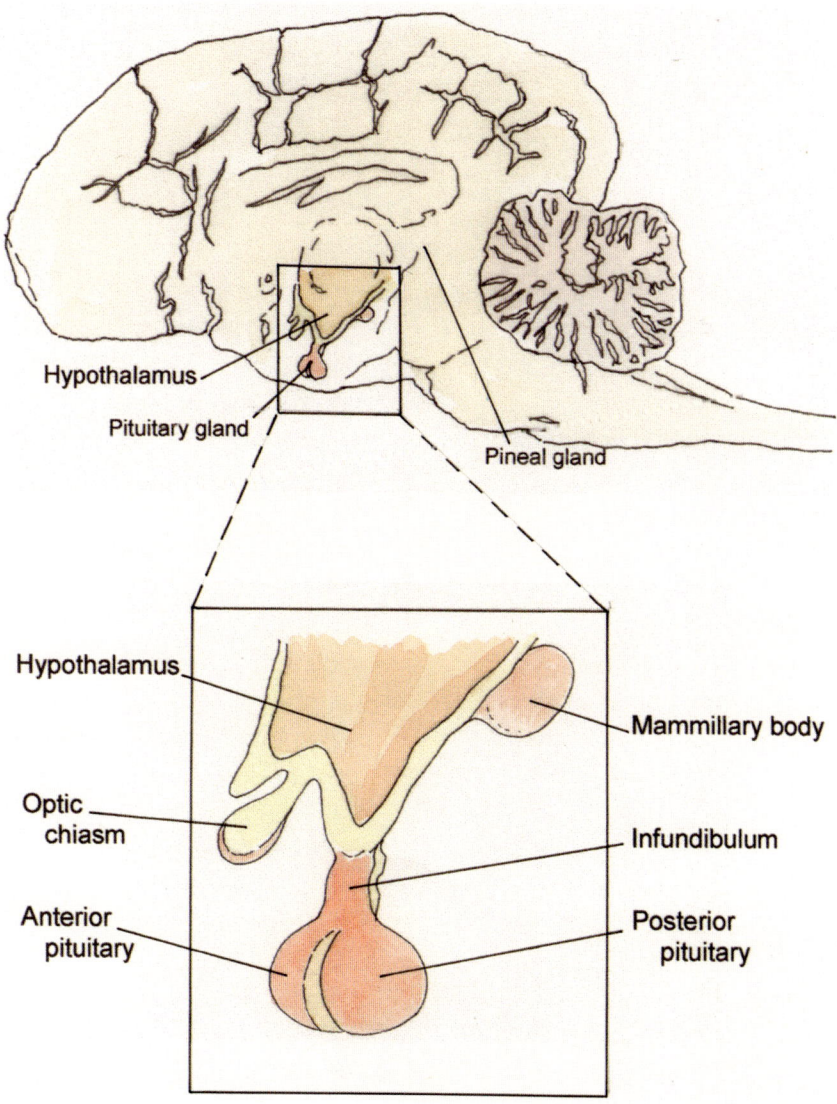

Hypothamus.

Canine Cognitive Skills

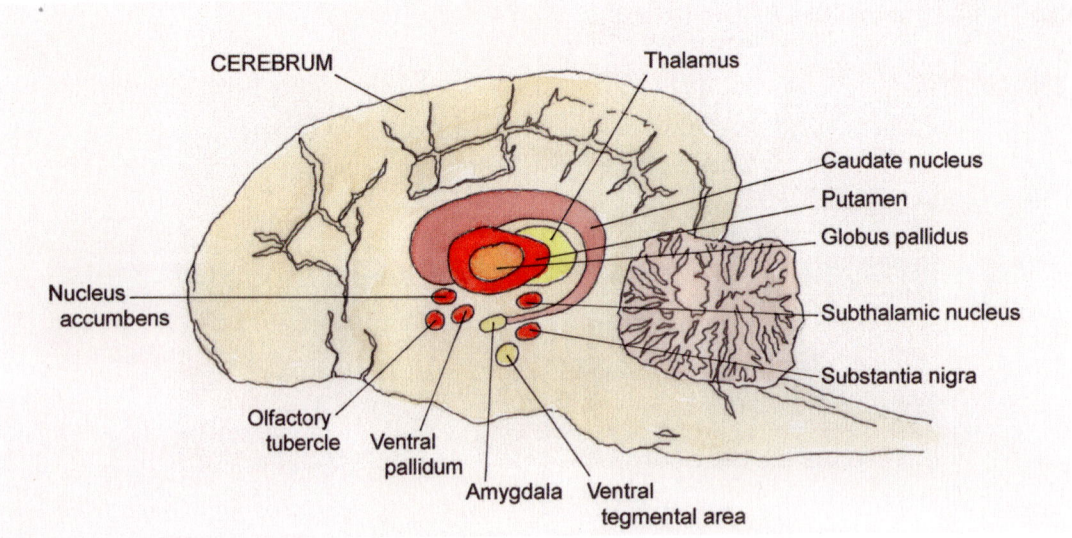

Basal ganglia.

MEDULLA OBLONGATA
This connects from the base of spinal cord; it is the first part of the brain to develop in puppies prior to birth.
Responsible for:
- Automatic functions, such as heartbeat, breathing, and blood pressure.
- Controlling function of the heart and lungs.

HIPPOCAMPUS
This plays important an important role in the consolidation of information from short-term memory to long-term memory.
Responsible for:
- Memory.
- Navigation.
- Limbic (emotion) and autonomic nervous system (unconscious functions).

HYPOTHALAMUS
This links the nervous system (signalling system) to the endocrine system (chemical messenger system) via the pituitary gland (see *page 9*) by means of hormone release.

Responsible for:
- Regulating hormone release.
- Appropriate behavioural responses – because it controls hormone production, it regulates body functions such as emotional responses and body temperature.

BASAL GANGLIA
The basal ganglia is situated at the base of the forebrain and top of the mid-brain. Neuroscientists have traced habit-making behaviours to this part of the brain; it also plays a key role in the development of emotions, memories and pattern recognition.
Responsible for:
- Voluntary motor control: These are movements we choose to make. For example, reaching for a glass of water from a table or, for a dog, choosing to step through a ladder instead of stepping on the rungs. This also relies on perceptual input – that is, judging the space between ladder rungs and where to place each foot. In other words, movements are thought out and planned in advance of the movement occurring.

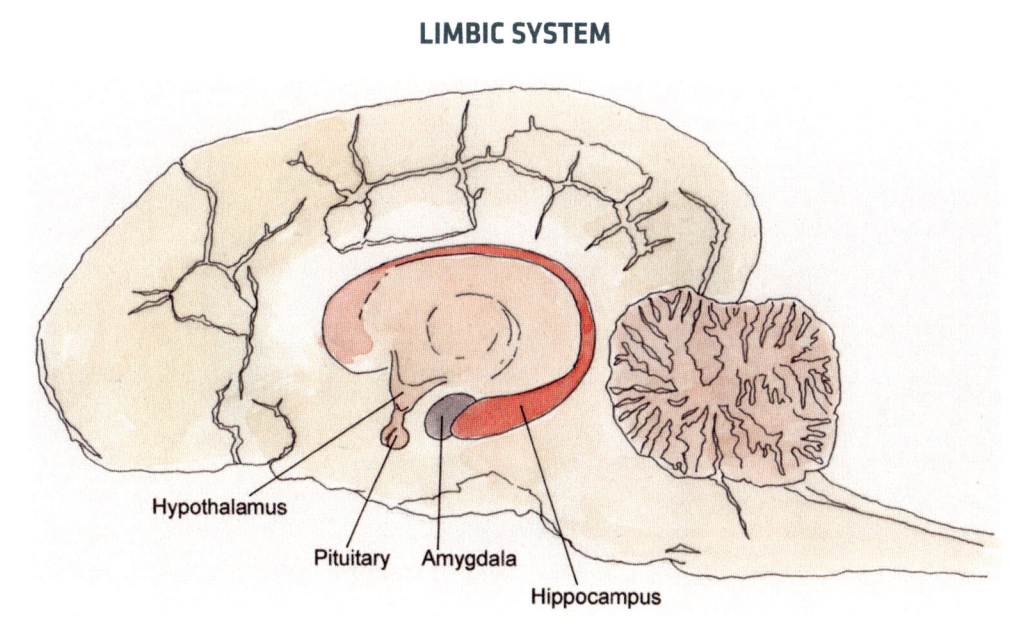

The limbic system is often incorrectly classified as a cerebral structure but, in fact, it is made up a series of structures which interact with various parts of the brain. These interactions influence motivation and learning, emotions, and memory.

- Procedural learning: This involves practical skills, such as finding out how something works and remembering how to use it next time. In dog terms, this might involve learning how to use a feeder or an enrichment toy where the dog has to learn how to 'work' the equipment so that the treats drop out.
- Cognitive and emotional functions: Cognition and emotional processes work closely together to form impressions, and the behaviour that results as a consequence. We rely greatly on this process, i.e., making use of positive associations, when we are attempting to change a dog's behaviour. For example, if a dog is concerned about a dustbin, we would give him high value, scrummy treats every time he is near the bin, or when it is in his eyeline. Good things happen to him when he is near the bin so he starts to associate good things with the bin. This, in turn, floods his brain with hormones that make him feel good instead of feeling fearful or concerned.

NEURAL PATHWAYS

As we can see, the brain is a complex organ with multiple functions. However, the different parts of the brain do not exist in isolation – they communicate with each other. Information travels via the nerve cells (neurons) of the brain which send electrical or chemical signals from one region of the brain to another. There are different types of neurons:

- Motor neurons that control muscles and movement.
- Sensory neurons that control sight, sound etc.
- Inter neurons that connect other neurons and interpret the information received.

This is made possible by neural pathways, which serve as communication channels in the brain. These can be compared to the paths in a forest. If we keep taking the same route through the forest, we will tread down the vegetation so that it is readily identifiable as an established route. Or, looking at it in terms of brain function, we are creating a new neurological pathway using the new route/behaviour instead of the old one. This then becomes a default behaviour, meaning it becomes a 'go to' behaviour in certain situations. However, we should bear in mind that if we eradicate habitual/pre-existing behaviour, it is inevitable that something will replace it.

For example, if you try to stop a dog jumping up and you fail to put something else in its place, such as a sit as the default behaviour, the dog will find something to replace it. This could be more jumping up – not just when you arrive home, but at strangers and in all scenarios – or he may start barking in frustration because of the increased emotional stimulation.

Consider the example of a dog who continually scratches at the door to be let out. You could put something in the way of the door so he can't scratch it, but that won't stop his desire to do the behaviour. Therefore, you would have to train an alternative behaviour – for example, he could ring a bell on a cord to signal that he wants you to open the door.

So, if we want to change habitual behaviours, it is good practice to make desired default behaviour the *new* habitual behaviour. For example, if you want to establish eye contact in training (because you can't teach a dog who is not looking at you), you will need to create a new neural pathway with this new behaviour. The first default behaviour to establish is the dog looking at you, followed by a 'sit' which will be an automatic reaction that does not require a verbal or a visual cue.

The difference between habitual behaviour and decision-making behaviour is choice. Consider what will happen if you want to stop biting your nails. While you are thinking about not biting your nails, you won't do it. However, it is a habitual behaviour which means the neurons in your brain are firing around the same neurological pathways. Therefore when your attention is elsewhere, you will suddenly become aware that you are biting your nails. Habitual behaviour has no thought or planning process. In contrast, decision-making behaviour has both planning and thought processes associated with it.

COGNITIVE LEARNING

This is a type of learning that focuses on maximising the brain's potential; it applies equally to humans and animals (in this case, dogs). It makes it easier to connect new information with existing ideas and this has a positive effect on both memory and retention. The cognitive learning theory explains how both internal (intrinsic) and external (extrinsic) factors influence mental processes to supplement learning.

INTRINSIC FACTORS

These are factors that are peculiar to the individual and, depending on the situation, they can have either a negative or a positive effect on training. Factors, such as health, ageing, emotions, and past experience, will affect individuals differently and will impact on learning, memory, focus and motivation.

Health and ageing

Both humans and dogs are equally affected by ageing which is evidenced by:
- Memory loss – it takes longer to recall things.

UNDERSTANDING THE CONCEPT

Instead of reinforcement coming from boisterous play, the dog learns through counter conditioning to default to his guardian – the predictor of good things.

- Inability to multi-task.
- Decrease in focus and motivation.

In addition, both dogs and humans suffer from dementia, which has a major effect on brain function.

Emotions

It is now well documented that animals experience a range of emotions that are comparable with our own. They are affected by fear, anger, stress, love, joy, etc., and we have to become expert at reading their body language and signalling in order to understand how they are feeling. As emotions drive behaviour, we must consider them as an important part of training and behaviour modification.

Counter conditioning is a technique used in training where we can change the way a dog feels in order to make a change in the behaviour offered. For example, if a dog barks and lunges at a refuse bin, it is fair to say that fear is driving his behaviour. So in order to change the behaviour, we have to address the emotion he is experiencing. So, if the dog is not frightened of the refuse bin, he will no longer bark and lunge at it.

On a social level, consider the example of an over-friendly dog who runs up to other dogs and greets them in an over-the-top manner. He thinks that all the fun comes from other dogs, but he is in danger of getting into trouble as his exuberant behaviour could trigger an aggressive response. We can change this behaviour by making other dogs the predictors of good things coming directly from his guardian – and not from other dogs. This means he will behave differently when he sees other dogs and default to his guardian instead.

Cognitive bias
Cognitive bias reflects mistakes in thought processing that can lead to inaccurate outcomes. For example, a dog's perception of a situation, a person, or another dog may be shaped by past experiences, or his own emotional state, and his resulting behaviour may be misguided or inappropriate. In a training scenario, it has an impact on performance as the dog is focusing on incorrect information, and overlooking what may be relevant to the task. This can lead to a state of learned helplessness, where a dog becomes so disheartened after continually failing in trials, and not receiving reinforcement, that he gives up trying.

Cognitive bias tests and learned helplessness models have shown that feelings of both optimism and pessimism occur in a wide range of species including rats, dogs, cats, rhesus macaques, sheep, chickens, starlings, pigs, and honeybees.

EXTRINSIC FACTORS
These are factors that happen outside the body, in the environment, and cannot be directly controlled. Outside spaces, boundaries, and objects are all classified as external factors and may impact on learning. For example, if you throw a ball for a dog in the park, he learns that going to the park may result in a game of ball. If you go to the woods with him, due to learned memory, he will not expect a game of ball.

Reinforcement also comes from an external source and, given that the reinforcer is something the dog values – food, a toy, praise/petting – it will have a motivating effect on his behaviour. He will work hard to get the reinforcement, and he is more likely to repeat the behaviour on future occasions in the hope of getting reinforcement.

COGNITIVE SKILLS

Cognitive skills are the essential qualities the brain uses to think, listen, learn, understand and focus. For us humans, it is second nature to employ these skills – we are not aware that we are calling on them as we navigate the world around us.

Dogs *do* employ these skills, but others kick in as they are far more easily distracted than humans. For the most part, well trained dogs use their learned cognitive skills as a default. Once they are learned, they become habitual and are performed without thinking. In addition, dogs can use their natural ability to problem-solve, learning how to get the things they want or need, or finding ways to communicate their needs to their guardians.

Assistance dogs do this all the time. For example, a guide dog will move his guardian away from a low-lying branch; a dog assisting someone with physical disabilities will load the washing machine as soon as the door has been opened.

In both humans and dogs, cognitive skills can be divided into five categories:
1. Attention.
2. Memory.

3. Logic and reasoning.
4. Auditory and visual processing.
5. Cognitive flexibility.

For each skill, the brain employs a different method to interpret and use information.

Human cognitive skills and/or skill sets, play an important part in processing information, whether new or known. This means that if even one of these skills (or skill sets) is weak, no matter what kind of information is presented to us, grasping, retaining, or using that information is seriously affected. In fact, most learning problems are caused by weak cognitive skills, which have a huge impact on behaviour. This is exactly the same for dogs!

Let us consider the five main skills and see how they impact learning:

1. ATTENTION

Learning cannot take place without focus and attention, a fact that applies to humans as well as dogs. This means ignoring all distractions and concentrating on the matter in hand, which is not easy. A human child needs to listen and pay attention in class in order to learn, just as a dog does in a training class.

There are different types of attention:

Sustained Attention: This is needed in order to maintain focus for an extended period

Paying attention requires the ability to focus and to filter out external distractions.

of time. Signs that sustained attention skills may be weak include jumping from project to project, and/or always being surrounded by unfinished projects. For dogs, an inability to sustain attention can be seen in breeds who are super busy and find it harder to concentrate on one task. They may attempt to deliver several other tasks at the same time as trying to deliver the cued task.

Selective Attention: The ability to ignore distractions and stay focused on the task in hand. Signs that selective attention skills may be weak include being easily distracted and/or jumping from task to task. You may already be thinking of a dog you know who has difficulty staying focused and ignoring distractions!

2. MEMORY

This involves both long and short-term memory:

Long-term memory: Long-term memory allows us to retain information for long periods of time, including information that can be retrieved consciously or unconsciously. In human terms, you may be able to remember the phone number from your family home, even if you haven't used that phone number in decades. This is known as 'explicit' memory which is based on factual recollection. For dogs, long-term memory might involve remembering the location of the water bowl, or which kitchen cupboard contains the treats.

Signs that long-term memory skills may be weak among humans includes forgetting names, things you used to know, and doing poorly in tests. For a dog it might mean forgetting simple, familiar tasks, evidenced by performing them more slowly while trying to remember.

Short-term memory: Short-term memory (storage) allows us to remember something for a very short period of time. For example, if a friend gave you their phone number, but you couldn't write it down, you would keep repeating it because you need to store in your short-term memory. The short-term memory of dogs is very short! In order for a dog to switch a memory from short to long-term, it would need to be practised repeatedly and consistently, otherwise it would be forgotten very quickly.

Working memory is an aspect of short-term memory. It lasts a little longer than short-term memory and is used when processing information. For example, you would use it to memorise instructions when working in a distracting environment. Signs of weakness in the working memory might be having to re-read directions in the middle of a task, experiencing difficulty following multi-step directions, or forgetting what was just said in a conversation. Dogs who struggle with working memory need to be given one task or cue at a time in order to be successful.

3. LOGIC AND REASONING

These cognitive skills allow you to reason, form ideas, and solve problems. For example, if you are given a riddle to solve, you need to think about it logically to find the correct outcome. When a dog is given an enrichment toy, for example, he needs to use logic and reasoning to find out how it works. He will explore the toy, trying different things until he is successful, i.e., he discovers how to release the treats.

Signs that a person may be weak in logic and reasoning skills may be frequently asked questions, such as: "What do I do next?" or saying: "I don't get this," and feeling overwhelmed by the task in hand.

We can see this during training sessions when a dog stops working and looks at the handler as if to say: "Help me, I need more from you". In these situations, help should be offered so the dog can be successful.

4. AUDITORY AND VISUAL PROCESSING

This involves using our senses – our hearing and our sight – as a means of processing information:

Auditory processing
In the human world, this means listening to a sound until we understand it. For example, if you have a voice message on your phone, which isn't very clear, you will listen to it several times in order to understand the message.

If a dog hears a new cue, he may offer a behaviour he already knows to try and earn the treat. When this fails to produce a treat, he will listen more carefully and work out what he needs to do to earn that treat.

Visual processing
In humans, this involves studying a picture of a visual situation until you have understood what is happening.

A dog uses visual processing when he watches you put something in a hiding place and then goes to get it a short time later. Signs of weakness may be the dog failing to remember things that were shown to him a short time ago, or needing a lengthy exposure to the visual image in order to retain it.

5. COGNITIVE FLEXIBILITY

This involves the ability to think, problem-solve, adapt, and adjust behaviour to suit an environment or situation. A weakness in this area means an inability to cope with change or to work effectively. Consider what would happen if Manchester United

Problem solving requires both logical thinking and cognitive flexibility.

were playing West Ham in a cup final and you, as a United fan, were surrounded by West Ham supporters. Would you cheer if United scored a goal? Unlikely, as that could lead to trouble. Instead, you suppress your behaviour to suit the environment, so much so, that if West Ham scored, you may even join in the celebrations with their supporters!

A dog who lacks cognitive flexibility may suffer from obsessive compulsive disorders, shadow chasing, or may struggle with switching from one task to another easily.

BRINGING ABOUT BEHAVIOUR CHANGE

Why can employing cognitive skills bring about changes in behaviour? The reason is that cognitive skills use different parts of the brain, overriding habitual functions, so default behaviour remains dormant. It is still present and accessible, but the brain is not 'thinking' about habitual behaviours because it is busy processing other things, especially if it is something that is fun to learn.

Consider the example of a dog who is fearful of other dogs. When he sees another dog, his default response it to feel anxious, a reaction that is triggered by the stress hormone, cortisol. However, when he is learning a new trick, and he is aware of another dog on the horizon, he abandons his default behaviour because he is concentrating on the task in hand, which he finds fun and enjoyable. His brain is being flooded with the feel-good hormones that make him feel happy and confident.

We can also facilitate behaviour change by giving the dogs the support and training they need. This is particularly the case when dealing with reactive dogs, and those who become frustrated in learning situations.

REACTIVE DOGS

In my lengthy experience I have found that reactive dogs are able to take part in cognitive skills exercises, in the presence of other dogs or people, as long as they feel safe and as long as their triggers are at a safe distance.

When we are anxious about something, the closer it gets, the more reason we have to feel concerned. This fear can build very quickly and eradicate the ability to think at speed, if at all. If we can remain at a 'safe' distance, we may be concerned, but we are still able to function. It is exactly the same for dogs.

As previously discussed, neurological pathways are created within the brain – communicating from one part of the brain to another – when we (or our dogs) are learning something new (see *page 11*). Neurons are firing away, creating new pathways in place of the habitual communication channels. There may be a stray neuron that shoots down the old pathway to a reactivity behaviour, which is why you might see a little of the 'old' behaviour. But this is typical of all habits; 'old' behaviour can rear its head when you least expect it.

So, in the case of the reactive dog, learning a new trick involves using a different part of his brain to problem-solve and thereby establishing a new neural pathway, rather than the habitual neural pathway that would lead him to react. The focus on the problem-solving task is more powerful than the presence of trigger because he feels good, and this acts as reinforcement. Being in a constant state of alert and worry is very disruptive so, if you feel better about something you are doing, you will choose this option. If this can work in a class environment, it can work in the park, the street or anywhere where the dog has triggers and/or a behaviour issue.

FRUSTRATION TOLERANCE

Training impulse control, self-control and frustration tolerance is important. Just like us, dogs are not born with impulse control and built-in tolerance frustration skills. These are skills that are learned through life experiences and, just like humans, adult dogs that have not developed tolerance to frustration and impulse control, may revert to undesirable behaviours, often taking the form of aggressive displays.

But what is frustration tolerance and, more importantly, how can dogs be taught the necessary coping skills so that they grow into well-adjusted adults? Frustration is the internal feeling of annoyance when you are upset because you can't have something, change something, or work something out successfully or at a speed.

Education starts within the nest, learning from both mother and littermates. The basic lesson is: *"you can't always have what you want, when you want it!"* This is a lesson we *all* must learn, albeit sometimes the hard way. But nevertheless, it is a life skill we have all had to learn one way or another.

Frustration often starts at a very low level and, if not addressed, can escalate quickly into negative, undesirable behaviour. Dogs

UNDERSTANDING THE CONCEPT

express frustration in a variety of ways, such as scratching, vocalising, yawning, chewing, licking, fidgeting, pacing, whining, barking and mouthing. These are all typical examples, but frustration can also manifest in any other types of behaviour pertinent to the personality of the dog in question.

Tolerance to frustration can be developed by employing a dog's cognitive skills. For example, you can teach a dog to 'ask' for the things he wants or values by using the 'sit to say please' protocol. This could involve the dog sitting in the following situations:
- When he wants the crate to be opened so he can go in or out.
- At mealtimes.
- When waiting to be given a toy/treat.
- Instead of jumping up.
- When he needs your help (to get something he cannot reach or find).
- When he wants to play.

Using this protocol, the dog learns that he can have the things he wants or needs; all he has to do is sit and he will get them. Dogs will always opt for the quickest way to reinforcement (regardless of what that is), so the dog will readily choose a 'sit' if this fast tracks him to a reward. The act of sitting generally involves giving eye contact and, as looking goes in tandem with listening, the dog is ready to learn.

Coping with frustration is a skill that needs to be learnt.

GAMES TO ENHANCE COGNITIVE SKILLS

Over the years, conducting my own research and hosting workshops, I have isolated the cognitive skills that are used in the games I have devised, and their lasting consequences:

Cognition skills	Games/Exercises	Results
• Working memory	• Foundation indicators	• Sustained attention/duration
• Long-term memory	• Confidence building	• Speed of processing
• Perception	• Focus and attention skills	• Frustration tolerance
• Visual processing	• Problem-solving	• Anticipation
• Recognition	• Match and sample	• Listening skills
• Logic and Reasoning	• Big and small	• Confidence boost
• Speed of processing	• Discrimination	• Self-management
• Auditory processing	• Counting	• Decreased reactivity
• Improve executive functions	• Short-term memory	• Motivation
• Preserve cognitive health	• Picture recognition	• Cognitive flexibility
	• Listening skills	

In the following chapters, we will look at strategies that will help you to enhance your dog's cognitive skills through the use of reward-based reinforcement. We will then move on to the foundation skills that you will both need to develop in order to get the best from the games I have devised. For ease of use, I have categorised the games in terms of the learning that is required, starting with beginners, progressing to greater challenges, and culminating in a master class designed for advanced dogs.

Chapter Two
REINFORCEMENT STRATEGIES

When we are training our dogs, we offer a reward as 'payment' for a job well done. It is a 'thank you' to the dog for carrying out our wishes/instructions. From the dog's perspective, the reward reinforces the behaviour he has offered so he is motivated to keep offering it, or to try something new in the hope of getting a reward. However, the reward must be something the dog wants *at that moment in time* and, contrary to popular belief, it does not always have to be edible. Dogs can be rewarded with food, play, verbal praise or tactile petting. It is all about what the individual dog perceives as being rewarding at that particular moment.

We also need to understand what is motivating a dog's behaviour. For example, a dog does not pull on a lead to eat chicken, cheese or sausage. He pulls because he wants to move in a particular direction so *that* is what he mostly wants at that moment in time. Therefore, movement is the reward you should give your dog when he stops pulling. Teaching a dog how to get what he wants is the key to successful training.

WHAT DOES YOUR DOG WANT?
To train your dog successfully, you need to tune into his personality and discover his likes and dislikes and which things (as there may be few or many) that he perceives as rewards and, more importantly, when (i.e., in what situation) he finds these things rewarding. For example, if you have been busy and you have not had time for a cup of tea, the very first cup you have will be a huge reinforcer: *"Ahhh lovely...."*. But the second cup will not be as rewarding as the first. Just

The key is to find a reward your dog truly values.

because the first cup was a reward, does not mean that *all* cups of tea are rewards. But *when* and *where* you received, or drank that cup of tea, could make it so.

Just like us, dogs have different needs and different preferences. Some are motivated by food, some are passionate about toys, and there are those who prefer interactive play. A small thing, such as the manner in which a reward is delivered, can make a difference. Gibson, a Jack Russell x Basenji I worked with, loved his ball. His greatest reward was to be given his ball to hold, or rolled for him to chase. He would even refuse a chunk of chicken and wait for the ball to be presented.

It is difficult to train a dog without knowing what will motivate him and how he will respond to stimuli. Both humans and dogs respond to internal stimuli – those that occur within the body, such as hunger and thirst, and external stimuli which is a response to stimuli outside the body, such as pain. For example, we humans share an in-built/internal response to dilate our pupils in response to light, or get goose bumps when we are cold. Our response to an external stimuli might be withdrawing a hand when we touch something hot.

Dogs share some of our in-built responses. For example, they dilate their pupils in response to light, but some are very different. For example, dogs have an in-built response to salivate when they see someone eating – just like Pavlov's dogs. An eternal response to stimuli would be a dog who wags his tail when he sees his guardian in the morning.

We also need to understand our dogs as emotional, sentient beings, if we are to be effective trainers. It is now widely recognised that dogs experience a wide range of emotions, just like us, so we need to become expert at observing their body language and facial expressions so we can find out how they are feeling and adapt our training accordingly.

THE QUESTION OF PUNISHMENT

This is a hot topic in dog training, and always provokes a highly emotional response. We all want to train our dogs using positive, reinforcing methods, but we also have to accept that learning involves both reward and punishment. For example, a child is told:

"If you don't eat your vegetables, you cannot have a dessert!"

It is a punishment because the child cannot have something he/she wants, unless they co-operate. It is unpleasant, but it is not a physical punishment. Positive/force free trainers use the same tactics, focusing on reward and non-physical punishment, i.e., a reward involves giving the dog what he desires at that moment in time, punishment involves removing what he desires at that moment in time.

For example, If I am holding a treat and I ask the dog to sit and he fails to do so, I withhold the treat until he co-operates. Then, when he *does* sit, I give him the food straightaway. This teaches him that if he doesn't do as I ask, there will be no reward until he performs the requested behaviour.

Effective trainers have no need to use force, to intimidate, or to provoke fear, because they know how to help dogs perform the desired behaviour. Force, intimidation, and fear may get results but the dog is not co-operating because he *wants* to, but because he feels he *has* to. Inevitably, there is a fall out, which could be a deterioration in the dog's behaviour, or in the relationship between dog and trainer. It could create a timid or unpredictable dog; a dog who finds it difficult to learn or trust. Some dogs suppress their behaviour in order to avoid punishment, but when an opportunity presents itself – such as meeting another dog – they will release their pent-up aggression. In contrast, force-free training promotes full compliance from the dog because he wants to participate. Working for rewards creates happy, puzzle-solving family members who have no need to suppress behaviours or adopt coping strategies.

Employing a psychological approach can, therefore, make it easier to train a dog in what we all agree is the preferred way – force free and providing choices. There is now scientific evidence which proves that dogs trained using non-aversive methodology (no pain, intimidation, force or fear), not only find the training highly pleasurable, they are also far more likely to be successful. Remember, reinforcement is key: what gets rewarded, gets repeated. A dog who knows he is working for rewards will be happy to learn – and to keep on trying until he gets it right.

UNDERSTANDING REINFORCERS

Understanding reinforcers is important if you want to appreciate how dogs learn. Food rewards are easy to give and, in most cases, they have a fairly instant effect so, understandably, we tend to rely on them. However, as already highlighted, a dog does not always perceive an edible treat as being rewarding. He may not be feeling hungry, you may be offering something he does not like, or it may be that he has other

HAPPY HORMONES

When we are participating in something pleasurable, the brain produces 'happy hormones' which influence how we feel and behave. The same is true of dogs. Therefore, if we can help a dog produce these brain chemicals, we can influence behaviour and bring about a change in behaviours we want to eradicate. The hormones include:

Serotonin: Helps to balance mood and promotes feelings of wellbeing and, therefore, has a huge impact on cognitive behaviour and skills. We produce serotonin when we exercise, which makes us feel good. Dogs produce it when we play with them or do things with them that they really enjoy.

Dopamine: Dopamine is associated with enjoyable activities, such as training and playing. It is also associated with rewards – those that are received, and also in anticipation of rewards to come. Therefore the link between dopamine and positive reinforcement is a great help to dog trainers as it increases willingness and compliance.

Endorphins: Released during exercise making dogs feel happy and energetic. They also help the body to cope by relieving pain and reducing stress.

Oxytocin: Strictly speaking, this is not a happy hormone, but it plays a key role in behaviour because it promotes feelings of positive emotion, bonding and social interaction – friendships if you like.

preferences, such as playing with toys or receiving tactile attention.

In my experience, it is not just the reward (treat) that acts as a reinforcer during the exercises I set up; there are other intrinsic reinforcers, such as taking part in the training and receiving audible rewards in the form of verbal praise: "you are a good dog", "you are so clever", "well done, good boy" etc.. Sometimes just doing something that is entirely different, such as using different equipment, can be rewarding. For example, if I use items in training that a dog has never seen before, it creates happy hormones, mainly dopamine, because he anticipates that something good is about to happen.

Dogs learn by making associations – both positive and negative. Therefore, a reinforcer is not simply a reward, such as food or play, it is the task associated with the reinforcer because it makes the dog feel good. In human terms, think of bubble wrap. You may be one of the many people who like to pop each bubble individually, because you find it satisfying. There is no reward at the end when all the bubbles have been popped because it was the enjoyment of popping them that was rewarding. If I was to give you a chocolate (or whatever treat you really like) after you had finished, you would take it, but it has no bearing on the task; it is an additional bonus.

The power of association: The task associated with the reward becomes reinforcing in its own right.

Reinforcers are divided into three categories:

PRIMARY REINFORCER
These are natural, 'unconditioned' reinforcers which a dog mechanically values, such as food, water or shelter; he does not have to learn their value. Some primary reinforcers are exclusive to a dog's breed. For example, the water retrieving gundog breeds love to swim and will often seek out water when they are being exercised.

In training, we make use of food as a primary reinforcer, motivating dogs to participate. However, some breeds – such as Border Collies and other breeds that are stimulated by movement, particularly chasing and stop and start movements – would prefer a secondary reinforcer (see below).

SECONDARY REINFORCER
A secondary reinforcer is a conditioned reinforcer. It is a learned behaviour that the dog knows and enjoys. It can be playing with toys, getting verbal praise, a round of applause, etc. The value of a secondary reinforcer is dependent on the environment, and how such an environment will influence the dog in question.

It is important to bear in mind that, just like us, the experience of learning a new task, whether it is positive or negative, will be logged in a dog's memory and from that point onwards, he will experience that emotion when he is asked to carry out that particular skill. If he loved learning it, he will want to repeat it, he will want to keep on learning, and love it forever! However, if the learning experience was stressful, the exercise in question will always conjure up a negative association.

TERTIARY REINFORCER
A tertiary reinforcer is anything that the dog already knows and loves to perform. It is based on cues that direct the dog, making him excited to perform a particular task. It is similar to a secondary reinforcer, which uses cues or commands to request a dog to perform a behaviour, but it also involves making use of associated positive emotion because the task is enjoyable for the dog.

For example, a tunnel may be a tertiary reinforcer for an agility dog. He is not motivated by the reward he will get for going through the tunnel, it is the act of going through the tunnel that he finds rewarding. Therefore, being cued and allowed to go through the tunnel is a huge reinforcer.

When we train dogs, we start with a chosen reinforcer to motivate the dog not only to take part, but to want to repeat the task. Then, we have to figure out a way to wean the dog off reinforcement. For example, when you are working on an exercise you don't want to keep feeding your dog for each step because he will get fat and this is detrimental to his health and wellbeing. In addition, he may not learn to carry out all the steps of an exercise for one treat as he will be expecting a treat every step of the way.

Let's consider the example of training a dog to go around a pole, pick up a toy and place it in a box, and then go to a bed to lie down. You would start training each step individually:
- Go round a pole.
- Pick up a toy.
- Place it in a box.
- Go to a bed and lie down.

Once you know the dog can do the individual behaviours, you can start to link them together to create a chain of events.

However, if you continue to treat the dog after each event, he will stop and wait for reinforcement before moving on to the next behaviour. So, to link the chain, you will need to cut out the first treat, which was the reward for going around a pole, before picking up a toy. This links two behaviours. Once the dog is proficient, you can delay the reward until the dog has picked up the toy and placed it in the box, and so forth.

But if the dog is rewarded by the task itself, fading out reinforcement is unnecessary; the task has become a tertiary reward.

Unlike, primary and secondary reinforcers, a tertiary reinforcer is all about creating a behaviour which generates fun for the dog. He picks up a cue and performs the given task because he enjoys performing it and it makes him feel good. Over time, the experience of carrying out the task has such a positive association, he will perform it without being cued to do so. He loves the task, and the fun, playful approach you have adopted will have a positive effect on his wellbeing – and on your training success.

When devising games to promote cognitive skills, I have made full use of tertiary reinforcers to make training enjoyable, build confidence and to improve the rate of success. In fact, a successful outcome can be a tertiary reinforcer as the dog is excited to perform that particular task.

WORKING WITH DIFFERENT REINFORCERS

If you use a combination of primary, secondary and tertiary reinforcers, you will find that your training becomes flawless and flows easier at each session. The dog will be

Changing reinforcers – and suiting the reinforcer to the task– will facilitate learning.

motivated and an intelligent use of reinforcer will aid his performance. For example, if a dog lacks motivation for a task, you can up the value of a treat from kibble to something the dog is passionate about, such as cheese or meat, which will add value to performing the task. However, if the dog is so excited about the prospect of a high value reward it affects his performance, you would drop the value of the reward.

Remember, the use of tertiary reinforcers means you can phase out food, as the dog likes to perform the task requested of him.

THE THREE-WAY ROUTE

Reinforcement is a three-way route.
It involves:
1. An edible treat.
2. Verbal praise.
3. Feeling good as a result of enjoying the task.

In training scenarios, a dog will often make a conscious choice about which reinforcer he prefers. For example, some dogs in my classes stop eating treats because they are not the primary reinforcer *at that moment in time.* It is the reaction – perhaps the pure joy – of their guardians that is a natural reward. It drives the dog – and guardian – to repeat and grow together, which then becomes a fourth reinforcer!

A dog might perceive working, and taking part, as the driving force (reinforcer), and is willing to repeat a task again and again when directed. Or, perhaps, he wants praise when successful or, indeed, a piece of his favourite liver sausage. I have also had dogs in my classes who are happy to take boring biscuits as a treat. For them, the real reward is taking part, so it is the exercise itself which increases the value of the treats. You may have heard it said that in order to get the best work from a dog, you need to pay top dollar. I say this is not always the case. We may go the extra mile for a financial reward, but we may do a better job because we enjoy the task, and we relish the praise we will get for achieving our goal. It is just the same with dogs.

When playing cognitive games with a dog, there may be several rewards that come into play:
- The game itself.
- The treat.
- A successful outcome.
- The trainer/guardian's reaction when the dog gets it right.

All of these rewards generate 'happy hormones' (see *page 23*) which make the dog feel great while he is playing the game and, as a result, motivate him to continue and/or try harder. Hey! That could be another form of reinforcement – "*I do it because it makes me feel good!*".

For the dog, the learning experience involves finding a route to reinforcement and/or the fastest route to reinforcement, whichever form that might take. Therefore, the trainer's task is to discover what makes a dog happy, which will not only increase motivation, it will also have a noticeable effect on accuracy.

YOUR VERY OWN THREE REWARDS

Training is all about finding what your dog finds rewarding. However, in our desire to find something the dog really values – his favourite food treat, or a particular toy or game – we are in danger of losing sight of the three rewards we carry with us all the time, namely:
- Voice: Talking to the dog and praising him.
- Touch: Stroking and petting.
- Eye contact: Looking at your dog is also perceived as a reward.

Don't forget, you also have a value!

All of the above are immediately available reinforcers which can be used to encourage a dog to repeat a behaviour, or to try something new. When you have no toy or treat available, or any other reward, you can use one of these valuable reinforcers instead, or in the interim. In fact it may well be that your dog does not require an additional reward, which makes *you* a primary reinforcer for your dog.

The other advantage of utilising your own three rewards, is that you can create a super reinforcer. You use one of them – looking at your dog – which is a pleasant reward for him, but if you use two at once – looking at him *and* talking to him – that is a bonus reward. If you use all three at once, adding in stroking and petting, that is a big, fat bonus for the dog; it is something he will relish and he will want to keep getting. This is powerful, so make sure you save the big, fat, bonuses for when you really need them!

RATES OF REINFORCEMENT

This refers to the frequency and/or the amount of reward that is given. For example, if you are teaching a dog something new, and you see a glimmer of understanding, you would pay a high rate of reinforcement to inspire him to continue and keep trying. Once the behaviour is stronger, you can drop the rate of reinforcement.

In the early stages of training, you would reward the dog every time he completed the task, employing a continuous rate

The rate of reinforcement should be high when a dog is learning something new, changing to a variable rate when learning is established.

of reinforcement. This consistency helps the dog to learn and understand the task. However, it is laborious and should be replaced by rewarding on a more random basis – a variable rate of reinforcement – once learning is established.

Remember, before you begin any training, whether it is practising something you have done before, something the dog is good at, or attempting to teach something new, you should always start by paying the dog – by which I mean rewarding him – for his attention. Initially, you should pay him well, using a high rate of reinforcement, and then reduce to a more variable rate once the behaviour is strong enough to do so.

Chapter Three
HOW TO TEACH COGNITIVE SKILLS

Over the many years I have been training dogs, I have always had a particular interest in finding out how their brain works, and how to develop their cognitive function. This has never been in sterile 'laboratory' conditions. I wanted to find ways of engaging both dogs and guardians in a way that was both enjoyable and beneficial in everyday life. To this end, I have devised a series of games that are based on a dog's inherent abilities. My aim was to encourage and develop these naturally occurring skills, allowing the dog to reach his potential. As already highlighted, this has great benefits for both dogs and their guardians, and it is the means of developing a really great bond between them.

I have categorised the games as follows:
- **Basic Cognitive Skills:** Starting easy and raising criteria.
- **Discrimination and choice**: Training the dog to make a choice and to indicate that choice to you.
- **Visual discrimination**: Looking at objects/items and learning from them.
- **Counting and patterns**: Involving focus and memory.
- **Big and small**: Making an informed choice relating to the size of objects/items.
- **Scent discrimination**: Choosing the correct 'target' scent.
- **Memory skills**: Alongside memory skills, adding a distraction or a request for a bridging behaviour.

The focus is on expanding a dog's knowledge and using his brain, which means the games and exercises are all low impact. They are, therefore, ideal for dogs recovering from surgery or illness or those that are in their later years, yet still need stimulation. Don't worry if you have limited space or you are training indoors, a 3m square is plenty big enough.

Take it slow, working at your dog's individual pace, so that he does not get frustrated or feel overwhelmed when he gets it wrong. Saying this, if you have set up the game correctly, wrong choices are quickly eradicated with the 50/50 choice set-up (see *page 34*).

TYPES OF LEARNING

Before embarking on teaching cognitive skills, we will first examine the different types of learning. This is something you may not have considered either for yourself, or for your dog. However, it is important to bear in mind that we are all individuals. One person will respond to a particular teaching style, while another finds it muddling. This is nothing to do with intelligence, it is about how the individual receives and processes information. It is similar for our dogs. For example, some dogs find it easier to learn in short bursts, so their training sessions should be short in duration and frequent. If a dog is struggling with a task, it needs to be broken down into small, bite-sized exercises so that he is learning a small part at a time. Then you can gradually join it all together to accomplish the whole task.

The various types of learning are:
Physical/Kinaesthetic learning: This is when you learn to do a task by physically doing it. You may read all about how to do it,

but until you actually *do* it, your learning experience will not be as effective and is unlikely to be retained. Dogs also benefit from this type of learning. If you keep repeating the task, you create a muscle memory which facilitates learning. Muscle memory is a motor skill which the brain turns into long-term memory for the task in question.

Auditory learning: Learning is more effective as a result of listening. Perhaps you learn better or just prefer to listen to a lecture rather than sit and read about the subject matter from a book. Dogs listen to the sounds and tones of cues in order to associate them with a function.

Visual learning: This is where the learner prefers images, colours and/or reading in order to learn. This type of learning involves memory skills to retain the things that you have seen in order to recall them from memory when required. Dogs observe the body language of humans and other dogs as a way of learning.

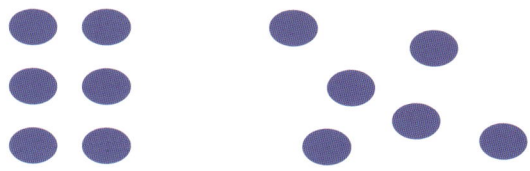
Both of these patterns have six dots. You don't have to count the spots on the left, but its more probable that you would need to count the spots on the pattern on the right to reach the correct total.

Verbal learning: In humans this involves written and spoken words. In dogs, it is connected to an auditory cue for an action, and is commonly known as associative learning. It is especially common in puppies, where it is credited as one of the main learning foundation skills.

Logical learning: This involves systematic learning, using patterns, numbers and other calculations to reach a goal. Logical learning in dogs is a more of an advanced type of learning. For example, learning patterns rather than counting to a particular number.

Let us consider the spots on a dice. We don't need to count the spots as the dice

Dogs learn by listening out for audible cues and by watching our body language.

lands as we have already learnt the pattern on each face of the dice.

Background Learning: As the name implies, this is a form of learning that goes on in the background subconsciously; it is more a memory type of learning. For example, you recognise a painting and you know you have seen it before. However, you can't remember where you first saw it. Then you discover that it is on a poster at a bus stop (which you never use) which is over the road from your office. You have never taken any notice of it, but you have absorbed the image using background learning.

Some of the games I have devised using cognitive skills also involve background learning. For example, while a dog is performing a task, he sees something but does not interact with it. Later, when I introduce that 'thing', it won't be completely alien to him because he has been seeing it in the background.

Dogs also learn from things that stress them, relax them and things they have seen, remembered, and copied.

THE EFFECT OF STRESS
When an individual – animal or human – is not experiencing stress, a balance exists in the cognitive memory system, allowing for the formation and recall of flexible memories. However, when that individual becomes stressed, it shifts the balance between underlying learning and memory.

Stress can have both a negative and a positive effect on learning. It has such a profound impact on our body chemicals, it can affect almost every organ in the body. If you have ever experienced stress, you may have noticed an elevation in your breathing, in your heartbeat, along with many other physical symptoms. Depending on what caused the stress and the duration of exposure, it could affect the way your brain processes the emotion, and have a lasting effect on your recall and your resulting behaviour.

A negative outcome is likely to occur if an acute stress is experienced repeatedly in a particular situation. For example, if a dog keeps meeting the same dog who always tries to attack him, he will develop a negative learning pattern associated with that dog, and maybe with other dogs, too.

A positive learning outcome would relate to stress that lasts for a short period, and has

> **THE THREE LS**
>
> As already highlighted, training cannot take place without the dog giving his attention and focus. This type of training has become something of a passion with me, and I now devote entire workshops it. This may sound like hard work but, believe me, both dogs and guardians have a lot of fun.
>
> My focus training is based on 'the three Ls:
> - Looking
> - Listening
> - Learning
>
> If a dog is looking at you, it generally means that he is also listening to you, which means he is ready to learn. To action the three Ls, I train a default sit, which is a sit that is not requested or cued verbally. It may be cued by the environment – for example, a dog may automatically sit when his food bowl is presented.
>
> I choose a sit because when a dog is in this position he is generally making eye contact, which encourages focus and attention. I refer to this eye contact as a default 'check in'. It forms the basis of a default question because when a dog is asked to sit, he is generally looking at you – asking what comes next – and if he is looking at you, he is listening to you, too!

the effect of increasing alertness and boosting performance. Animals in the wild that are hunted as prey learn positively from short bursts of stress, when being chased. They become uber alert and their ability to run is maximised in order to escape capture.

In the context of our domesticated dogs, positive stress can aid performance in a competitive environment. For example, agility dogs have to wait in line for their turn; they are fully aware of what they are waiting for – the opportunity to run. The wait can be a little stressful but it doesn't last long, and/or the sound of other dogs barking and getting excited can produce short bursts of stress which increases adrenalin. So when the dog enters the ring, there is a good chance that the short-term stress he has experienced will have a positive effect on his performance, being super focused and producing faster times.

MAKING CHOICES

Developing a dog's cognitive skills means encouraging him to use his brain to problem-solve and make choices. We are training him to think independently rather than simply responding to a set of instructions. However, as we have seen, a dog's brain works differently from a human brain and we cannot frame our training based on our own perceptions and problem-solving abilities.

For example, it would be so much easier if you could say to your dog: *"I am going to show you a picture and I want you to match it with the same picture that I have pinned on the wall, over there"*. But we cannot; it is not that simple.

Instead, we need to introduce choice using a process of elimination and manipulation, arranging the criteria and

In training, we 'guide' a dog to make correct choice, and to ignore the non-rewarding option.

guiding the dog through a series of steps to reach the desired goal. It is by working through this process that the dog learns there is a correct and an incorrect choice. He then learns to ignore the non-rewarding option (the incorrect choice) and choose the rewarding option (the correct choice). So, at this point, the dog's sole task is to work out what will pay, and avoid the options that will not pay – something dogs are very good at!

Note: If a dog makes an incorrect choice, it is vital to say and do nothing. If you make a 'ah-ah' sound or speak to him –"no, that's wrong, try again" – you will interfere with his natural thought process which means it will take him longer to arrive at the correct answer. However, if you say and do nothing he will go through the options – "no reward is being offered on that one so I need to choose the other one" – and, eureka, he gets a reward. If he repeats the incorrect move, the message of no pay day is repeated, which gives a further opportunity for learning. In addition, saying and doing nothing motivates the dog to keep trying because he has discovered that getting it wrong is not aversive in any way.

Remember, when teaching anything new, the key is to set up for success, as often as possible and as easily as possible. This could mean that you train the desired behaviour in the thinnest of slices and only increase the 'thickness' of each slice very gradually and only when you can see that your dog is ready for it. You also need to be confident that you, as a trainer, are ready to handle an increase in criteria.

LEARNING TO CHOOSE

In the early stages of cognitive skills training, there must only ever be two choices available. We offer the dog an alternative: this one or that one? This helps the dog to make associations, a learning process that dogs utilise both quickly and effectively. If the first choice is wrong, the other must be right, and vice versa. From the trainer's perspective, this involves a quick turnaround, offering an alternative after a wrong choice so the dog does not become frustrated and is motivated to keep trying. It also teaches both dog and trainer that mistakes are OK; it is simply a matter of moving on and trying something new.

The first step is to educate the dog so that he understands:
- He does have a choice.
- How to make that choice.
- How to communicate that choice.

Let us put this in a human context and consider a choice game involving playing cards.

You have a pack of playing cards, which are divided into four suits – clubs and spades, which are black; hearts and diamonds, which are red. There are 13 cards in each suit, showing numbers and pictures. By using a process of elimination, and asking the right questions, I could easily guide you to choose the card I want. So, if I want you to choose the two of clubs, which is black, I would ask a series of questions where there are only two possible answers to each question:

Question 1. "There are black suits and red suits in a pack of cards, isn't that right?"
You would have to agree with me because it is factually correct.

Question 2: What colour do you want to choose: red or black?
This is where the clever bit comes in. If you choose red (remember, I want black) it leads me to…

Question 3: "So that leaves us with black, doesn't it?"
Again, this is factually correct so you would have to agree. If you chose black – the correct choice – I would go with your choice and proceed to the next part of the process, where we need to eliminate a suit.

Question 4: The black cards are composed of two suits: spades and clubs. Which do you choose?
If you choose clubs, we have successfully eliminated a suit. If you select spades, I will proceed to…

Question 5: "So that leaves us with clubs, doesn't it?"
Do you see what is happening? It doesn't matter if you make the 'wrong' choice because I am guiding you down the road I want you to go. It may not be the route you think you are going on, but you still feel in control of your choices.

To reach my goal, I would whittle it down further, using the same process, and only offer two choices, so that one would be correct and one incorrect, until, eventually, you choose the right card: two of clubs (black). There you have it: discrimination and choice! Slicing behaviour into micro manageable pieces to arrive at your destination.

When I am playing games to develop cognitive skills in dogs, I always start by offering two choices, one correct, and one incorrect. If the dog makes the wrong choice, I simply keep going with the one that is correct. The dog will eventually ignore the incorrect option because there is no pay day. In contrast, when he makes the correct choice, I reward him with a treat or whatever he finds rewarding at that moment in time (see *page 23*).

A dog will find it easier to focus if you train in an environment that is as free from distractions as possible.

SETTING UP FOR SUCCESS

There are many ways where you, as a trainer, can facilitate learning and promote successful outcomes. The first consideration is the training environment, selecting a venue that has minimal distractions in the early stages of learning a new exercise (see Dealing with distractions, *page 37*). It is also important that there are no physical distractions, such as toileting requirements, or being hungry, thirsty, or tired, which will impact the learning process.

Make sure you always have a bowl of water readily available where you are training. Utilising the brain creates a thirst and water is a must for brain power to support brain plasticity, improved function, better memory, improved creativity, better problem-solving and increased concentration. It is also important to attend to your own needs so you can be at the top of your game. Remember, your brain will be active during the training and you will also benefit from hydration.

KEEP IT SHORT AND SWEET

Engaging the brain is tiring – for dogs and humans alike. Yet we are always tempted to keep going, doing too many repetitions, and making our training sessions too long. Instead of making progress, we are more likely to end up with the dog either switching off or feeling frustrated, not to mention the frustration we experience ourselves.

Training should be limited to short sessions, with exercises broken down into small, manageable steps. If your dog is struggling with a particular aspect, break it down into thinner slices. When you are confident that he is ready, you can gradually increase criteria. This will allow learning to take place and the new behaviour/skill will be retained in the dog's long-term memory. In this way, you are building a solid foundation of knowledge which will mean that you, and your dog, can progress confidently, successfully and without frustration. This method of teaching encourages dogs to love the challenge of learning the skills, and motivates them to keep trying.

TEN-TREAT TRAINING

To avoid the mistake of training for too long, adopt the ten-treat training method. Simply count out ten treats and once they have been used up, the training session is over or you stop work on this particular exercise and move on to something different.

PIPE DOWN!

We are all guilty of talking to our dogs too much when we are training them – not to mention the additional 'help' we offer in the form of signalling and body language. We are in 'alert mode', ready to give additional cues at any sign of hesitation. Obviously, if learning is to take place, the dog needs to be given instructions, but he also needs time to concentrate and process that information.

Observe your dog closely and when he goes into 'concentration mode' – watching you and listening to you, anticipating the next cue – you need to keep quiet! If you keep up a flow of instructions, it is highly likely that your dog will only hear the occasional cue in a blur of white noise. Inevitably, he will become confused which will interfere with his ability to learn and, consequently the likelihood of a successful outcome. It is estimated that an adult dog will think about what he has been asked to do for approximately 8-10 seconds before asking for help. We need to allow our dogs this vital thinking time so that they can find the solution themselves. This could be another

HOW TO TEACH COGNITIVE SKILLS

Dogs need the opportunity to process what is happening in the environment.

tertiary reinforcer for your dog (see *page 25*).

In the initial stages cognitive training is based on choice, allowing the dog to choose between two options. If he makes a choice, and you do not mark it or respond in any way, he will have a quick think about the silence and then he will automatically choose the other option. Again, if you speak or move during this period, you will interfere with his 'thinking time' and slow his response. It may have further negative consequences if the dog feels frustrated by the situation.

DEALING WITH DISTRACTIONS

Distractions are every trainer's nightmare! Why should a dog resist the temptation of enticing scents, or the possibility of engaging with other dogs because we want him to focus on learning a new trick? Getting a dog's attention, and keeping it, can be both challenging and stressful. Therefore, let us think outside of the box, and find new ways to keep our dogs focused and *wanting* our engagement.

Firstly, let's think in terms of working 'with' distractions, instead of against them. If your dog becomes distracted by something he has seen, or something that is happening in the environment, remember:

You only need to be proactive if your dog is being reactive.

In other words, it is not a criminal offence for a dog to be curious about something that is happening in the environment, but reacting to it may be. If a dog is simply looking at a distraction, he is not doing any harm. It may be that he is simply gathering information so he can find out that the distraction/happening is not to be feared. If you interrupt, how can he learn this valuable lesson? If he is allowed to keep on looking, he may progress to making a choice – an educated choice – such as deciding to move on. If you intervene, trying to shift his focus, you risk becoming an additional, secondary distraction. For example, if a dog is preoccupied by looking at a distraction, he will not be tempted by the treat you wave in his face – even it is a whole cooked chicken! Instead, he will try to dodge away from the food because it is getting in the way of the distraction that requires his focus.

So, try this instead. Imagine you are out for an on-lead walk with your dog and he becomes fixated on a distraction, such as another dog, a person, or a bird in a tree. Instead of trying to break his gaze, stop, stay still, be silent, and wait. The lead should be loose, allowing the dog to maintain his gaze. Ideally, you should stop as soon as you notice your dog becoming distracted. From then onwards, every step you take brings the dog closer to the point of distraction, which means he will become hyper focused and it will be harder to get through to him. If the distraction involves barking, lunging etc., the dog's response will increase in direct proportion to its proximity.

Allowing the dog to focus on the distraction, means he can soak up all the information he needs to assess learn, and cope, in his own time. Once he has seen enough and is satisfied that there is no more to gain from looking, he will either continue with his walk and his normal 'dog' behaviour, such as sniffing, or he may turn to look at you because you are standing still and quiet. If he makes the latter choice, which I call a 'welcome back' moment, I immediately offer a reward, which could be a piece of sausage, a game with his favourite ball, or just over-the-top praise. I want him to learn that being distracted is okay, but eventually it is boring because nothing happens. However, when he defaults back to me, he gets something he really likes *from me*, rather than from the environment. *Environment nil, guardian one!*

If you adopt this strategy you will notice, over time, that the dog no longer becomes so fixated on the things in the environment – be it dogs, people or wildlife – that he previously found so distracting.

So, what should you do if your dog gets distracted in the midst of a training session? For example, you are working on an exercise and everything is going great. Then, suddenly, the dog becomes distracted by a noise coming from outside.

As with environmental distractions, the best strategy is do nothing: stay still, be quiet and wait. Observe the dog closely, looking for the moment when he shifts focus from the distraction. This may be very subtle and very slight, but it is the moment to recapture his attention. If you try to talk to him, or re-cue him, when he is completely preoccupied, you risk poisoning your cue, whether it is one that is in his repertoire, or a cue you are trying to introduce. Worse still, he may learn to block you out.

The ability to block you out should be regarded as a skill. The more a dog practises it, the more successful he will become, so we need to be careful. To put it in a human context, imagine I am admiring the cakes in a baker's window and you stand in front of me in an attempt to stop me looking at them. I would naturally try to look over your shoulder, or dodge away from you so I can continue looking. Consciously, or unconsciously, I will block out anything you say to me because I am focusing all my energy on trying to look at the cakes, instead of simply taking an interest in them. The cakes become a primary distraction and you are a secondary distraction that I am trying to ignore, because the desire to look at the cakes has grown exponentially!

We have probably all witnessed the scenario of someone trying to get their dog's attention by proffering a piece of chicken, which he ignores because the distraction has the greater pulling power. I have lost count of the number of times I have been working with a client who says: "I could put a whole cooked sausage in front of my dog and he would still ignore me". Well, now you know why, and also how easy it is to train a dog to block you out when he is distracted.

If we wait the for the dog to become less distracted, we have more chance of success. Instead of learning to block you, he learns that nothing is more rewarding than giving you his attention. It also prevents us from becoming frustrated because the dog is not listening; we can now appreciate that listening when distracted is challenging work.

Timing is all important. You need to become proactive the moment you see the dog shift his focus – even slightly – from the distraction, and reward him with a 'welcome back' treat. Once you have his attention, you must make absolutely sure that something good happens. You are not only rewarding his response at that moment in time, but you are also future proofing so that he learns that looking at something interesting is not as rewarding as looking away from it to look at you. For example, if a dog sees a bird, he may look at it for a few seconds, and then turn to look at you because he has learnt that the bird has nothing good in store for him, but you do! He knows that every single time he turns away from a distraction and opts to look at you he will be given something he really values, whether it is his favourite toy, a game of chase as you run in the other direction, or a really scrummy treat that you know he adores.

Wait for that moment when your dog switches focus – away from the distraction – and then ask him to re-engage.

Chapter Four
FOUNDATION SKILLS

Before we start playing cognitive games, we need to establish a training methodology and then establish some basic foundation behaviours which will be used in the ensuing games. As already highlighted, my training approach is completely force free and gives the learner a choice (see *page 34*). If the choice is not my preferred choice, it is my job to change something about the environment, or the training itself, in order, to clarify what I want. This takes time and experience.

In general, I shape the behaviour, working progressively towards the desired goal. In general I prefer to use a marker word, in place of a clicker, to tell the dog he is performing the desired behaviour. But this would depend on the dog. I have also found that some students do better if they are not encumbered by a clicker, or if they are struggling with precise timing when using it. In this case, I would encourage the use of a marker word.

We then have to consider the choice of marker word. Personally, I don't like using 'yes' as it can be said in so many different tones. If a trainer gets carried away because training is going well, 'yes' can be high-pitched or even shouted, which could have a detrimental effect on the dog. I use 'good' as my marker word but, the choice is a matter of personal preference. But whatever word you use, the dog must understand that it means his behaviour is correct and a reward will follow, i.e., the marker word must be pre-conditioned.

Although shaping is my preferred method of training, I am always open to other methodologies depending on the requirements of the individual dog. That said, luring – using food to guide the dog into the correct behaviour – would be my least preferred option. Dogs who are lured to perform a behaviour, are unlikely to use cognition to learn and problem-solve. A dog who is lured waits to be told – lured – before acting. This can make him lazy as he has no need to 'think'; he will complete the task and get a reward simply by following a treat. Cognitive thinkers do not wait for hints, they attempt to find solutions right away. They are motivated learners!

WORKING FOR FOOD

When I am teaching foundation skills, and all subsequent cognitive skills games, I use food as a reward. As already discussed, the reward must be perceived as being valuable to the dog you are training, and all dogs have their own individual preferences. However, most dogs will work well for an edible reward as long as the food is perceived as a treat by the dog in question. If the dog is not food motivated, I would use a different reinforcer, such as play, but the disadvantage is that any game involving a toy is time sensitive. I would, therefore, start by using an interactive treat ball – where the treat is hidden inside – and then wean the dog from the treat ball to a food reward as soon as possible.

Remember, high value treats, such as cheese, chicken, or liver, motivate; low value treats, such as kibble, calm a dog when he has become too excited to process instructions and is thinking more about the treat as a final destination rather than

FOUNDATION SKILLS

concentrating on the exercise in hand. A low value treat is a tangible reward, but the dog is still able to think.

On a practical note, food treats should be easy to handle, i.e., not too sticky. In some of the exercises, the treats are thrown so they need to be the correct consistency, and they need to be clearly visible.

With practice, your dog will go to his anchor position on cue, and stay in position until he is released.

ANCHOR POSITION

Most of the games I have devised start with the dog in the 'anchor' position. This involves teaching the dog to use a bed, a mat, a crate or a low platform as a base where he is happy to settle until he is released. Work out whether your dog is more settled in a 'sit' or a 'down' and then teach him to go to his base, and adopt this position, gradually building the duration. Be generous with your rewards so the dog builds a really positive association with his base, and staying in position on his base.

Teaching an anchor position is invaluable in training. It allows the dog to stay calm, to focus and observe what you are doing. When you are ready, you can give his 'action' cue, which could be using his name to get attention followed by a cue, such as "show me", which tells him it is time to start work. It can also be used to reset the dog if he makes an error. You can send him back to his base and then ask him to try again. Finally, it provides a place for the dog to rest during training sessions.

I also recommend providing a pre-stuffed kong, which will encourage the dog to return to his base, and the activity of extracting food will give him an incentive to stay there. It is a way of keeping him entertained during breaks. The food you use depends on your dog's preferences; it can be as simple as his breakfast kibble or cream cheese. However, for this purpose, I advise stuffing the kong with something 'lickable', so that the dog remains stationary. When a kong is stuffed with solid food, it takes a bit of bashing and thrashing to extricate the contents. Lickable food encourages calmer behaviour.

VOLUNTARY EYE CONTACT

Without asking, we want the dog to look at us for direction, confirmation, guidance and/or security. I, therefore, teach a default check-in, which means the dog volunteers eye contact. This is invaluable as it ensures

Teaching voluntary eye contact enhances learning as the dog learns to 'check in' without being asked.

KAY9 CHICKEN CAKE RECIPE

I have a 'cake' recipe that I give to all my clients because it is easy to make, it freezes well, and dogs love it! I have made this recipe for many years and have yet to find a dog who doesn't like it. It is easy and very cheap to make – and you know exactly what is in it.

I reserve chicken cake for those moments in training when I need a high value treat in order to guarantee compliance, particularly if I am working with dogs that react to triggers. By using a very high value treat – and reserving it for very specific situations – the dog quickly makes an association that trigger equals high value, tasty treat. This motivates him to try hard and, at the same time, he will be producing hormones that will have an emotional impact on his response to his triggers.

I also use chicken cake when I am trying to create a new association. Again, if the dog only gets this very special, high value treat when he is working on a new exercise, or a new concept, it will have maximum impact. Homemade treats are the ultimate reward – your top dollar pay day!

Here is how to make chicken cake:

Ingredients
- A whole chicken (even better with giblets) or a bag of chicken carcasses from the butcher (mega cheap but still as good).
- Flour (as required).
- 1 egg.
- 2 cloves of garlic.
- Bicarbonate of soda (¼ tsp).
- A cup of milk
- 1 chicken stock cube

You can also add turmeric which is scientifically proven to have a number of health benefits.

Method
- Roast the chicken as per the cooking instructions.
- While chicken is cooking, mix the stock cube with boiling water and leave to cool.
- When the chicken is cooked, remove as much meat as possible. Cover and leave to stand.
- Using a large chopping knife, smash the remaining carcass (as is, skin and all) into small pieces and crush as many bones as possible.

---

you have the dog's attention without nagging or getting into the bad habit of using 'watch' when, in fact, you want a different behaviour.

To teach voluntary eye contact:
- Stand in front of the dog, who should be stationary in a sit or a down. When he looks up at you, mark his behaviour and drop a treat to one side.
- When the dog has eaten the treat, wait for him to look at you before marking and rewarding.
- Progress by taking a step away from the dog as he looks at you. If he maintains eye contact, mark and reward.

FOUR POINT ACTION PLAN

Choice is a major factor in training cognitive skills (see *page 33*) so when your dog makes a choice, he needs to be able to indicate it by showing you what he has chosen. This involves teaching the dog four basic behaviours:

1. **Tap:** Tapping a plastic lid with his paw.
2. **Touch:** Using a nose touch on an item, such as a piece of card.
3. **Push:** Pushing with his nose, instead of using his head or feet.
4. **Look:** Looking at piece of paper from a short distance, without interacting with it.

- Put the smashed carcass into a pot and add water so that it only just covers the carcass.
- Cover and simmer for two hours.
- Leave to stand until it is cool – a tasty jelly will collect at the bottom of the pan.
- Using your fingers, feel for and remove all bones and discard them. Keep the residual meat, skin and cartilage, and the lovely jelly that has been produced.
- Place the filtered carcass mass into a liquidiser/blender so that it becomes a smooth mush.
- Roughly chop the cooked chicken and add to the blender. (Keep some back to add in later if you want some chunky pieces of chicken in your treats).
- Add all the other ingredients except the flour.
- Now add the flour gradually until it resembles a cake mixture consistency. (If you kept back some chunky bits of chicken, add them to the mix and stir in).
- Line a baking tray with baking paper and add the cake mix. Spread out the contents evenly and bake until a skewer comes out clean. This should take approximately 30 minutes at a temperature of 190 degrees. Test and keep baking if required.
- When cool, slice the cake into small squares and bag up portions to freeze.
- If you want some extra crunchy treats, spread half of the chopped cake on a baking tray and return to the oven for approximately 10 minutes. I usually put the mixture back in the oven, but turn the oven off and allow the residual heat to dry the treats.

Using the above recipe, you can make a variety of different treats by substituting the chicken and stock cube for:
 – 1 pack of lamb's liver and lamb stock cube.
 – 2 tins of tuna and a fish stock cube.
 – 2 tins of salmon and a fish stock cube.
 – 1 packet of grated cheese and a vegetable stock cube.
 – Leftovers such as sausages, potatoes, other vegetables, and a vegetable stock cube.
 – Old packets of treats from the cupboard and a stock cube.
 – 1 tin of corned beef.

Once the dog has mastered these skills, he has the ability to show his choice. I use the cue, "show me" (see *page 48*). For example:

'Now that I have shown you a sample, "show me" your choice from selection of samples on the wall.'

In my cognitive skills workshops, I recommend that dogs should be a minimum of eight months before starting foundation work. By this stage, the brain is a little more mature and is equipped for problem-solving at this level. A dog's brain is fully developed at around two years of age, although learning capabilities are ongoing.

BASIC SET-UP
To teach the foundation skills and, going forward, the different levels of cognitive games, I use a basic set-up which includes the following items:
- Bed/crate/platform to use as the dog's base.
- Pre-stuffed kong.
- Cut up treats.
- Fresh drinking water for the dog.

ADDITIONAL EQIPMENT
This will be referenced in the step-by-step instructions for each game. It includes:
- The lid of a plastic container.
- A thick piece of card.

Canine Cognitive Skills

1. TAP

Objective: Using a paw to tap a plastic lid.
You will need: Treats, the lid of a plastic container.
Verbal cues:-
'Wait' – to ask the dog to wait and watch as you set up the exercise.
'Good' – verbal marker (or clicker if you are using one).
'Tap' – the cue for the desired behaviour.
'Go' – to invite the dog to start the behaviour.

Step-by-step

- Start by asking your dog to go to his base/anchor position and let him watch you as you place a treat on the floor.
- Hold the lid between your finger and thumb, and place it over the treat. Keep hold of the lid, otherwise the dog will push it around the floor with his nose instead of learning to use his paw.
- Release the dog from his base with your action cue. At this stage, use 'go' (or 'ok' if you prefer) and encourage him to come and investigate. Later, change the verbal cue to the one you are using for the desired behaviour. In this case 'tap'. Make sure the lid remains in contact with the floor, and hold it as still as possible so the dog cannot snuffle out the treat with his nose.

TRAINING TIP

It is important to withhold the verbal cue for a desired behaviour until the dog is actually doing it. If you use this cue too soon, you might erroneously be naming an error the dog is making while he is trying to work out what behaviour is required.

- When pushing with his nose does not work, the dog will try to move the lid with his paw instead. As soon as his paw comes into contact with the lid, you can name it by

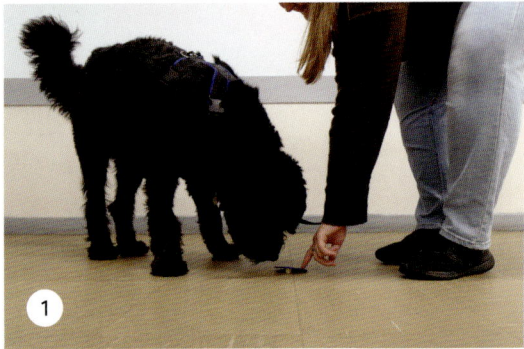

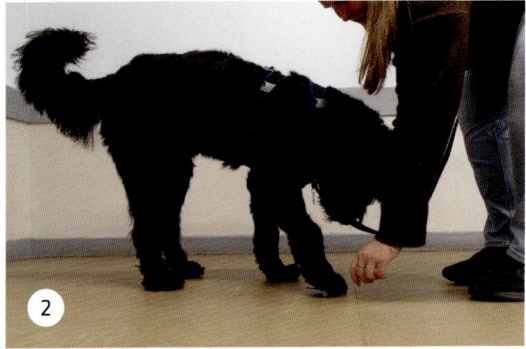

Timing is important with this exercise – wait until the dog is performing the behaviour correctly before giving the cue.

saying "tap", and then lift the lid allowing him to eat the treat.
- Repeat this several times until the dog opts to use his paw to tap the lid, thereby getting the treat, instead of using his nose to move the lid away from the treat.
- After a few trials with a good success rate, you will reach a stage when you no longer need to hold the lid as the dog is now targeting it with his paw.

SUCCESS RATES

Generally speaking it should be 'clearly above chance' at this stage – showing improvement – not perfect every time!

- Now place the lid on the floor, but this time, do not put a treat underneath it. Ask the dog to tap the lid. Wait patiently and allow him to process what you have asked him to do. As soon as the penny drops, and he taps the lid with his paw, mark and reward.

- When your dog is reliably performing the behaviour without placing a treat underneath it, you can start to add distance. Ask the dog to wait on his base, or any other place where he feels comfortable, and place the lid on the floor at a metre's distance from him. Repeat your 'wait' cue as you return to the dog's side, and then give his 'tap' cue.
- As soon as the dog has correctly targeted the lid, tapping it with his paw, mark it by saying "good" and put a treat on the lid. We want the dog to learn to tap the lid and stay there, so we make the lid the point of delivery for the reward. This gives the lid value and will, therefore, become the focal point of his attention.

2. TOUCH

Objective: A gentle nose touch on a piece of card.

You will need: Treats, a piece of thick card.
Verbal cues:-
'Good' – verbal marker (or clicker if you are using one).
'Touch' – the cue for the desired behaviour.

You may have already taught a 'hand touch' to your dog, where he puts his nose in the palm of your hand, on request. This behaviour is similar but now you are teaching him to touch an object, which is at some distance from you.

Step-by-step

- Start by holding a piece of card in front of you, but do not bring it towards the dog's face. The success of this exercise depends on the dog *choosing* to approach the piece of card. If you offer it – presenting it to his face – he will almost certainly back off, which is counter-productive to what you want to achieve. Indeed, he may stop trying all together!

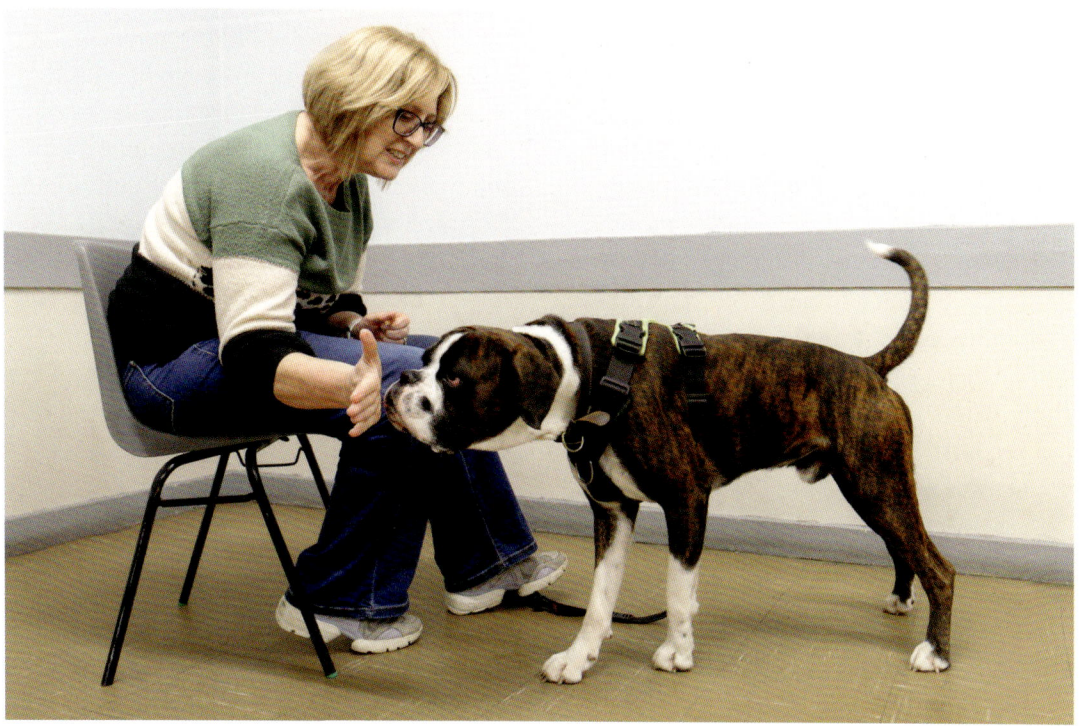

A hand touch is the basis of this behaviour.

- Keep absolutely still and do not look at the dog. Focus on the piece of card, say nothing, and wait. Give him that all important thinking time so that he can work out what he has to do, without interference. Bear in mind, there is nothing more annoying than someone butting in when you are trying to work something out, and you are on the brink of getting the right answer. Arrrgh!
- At the moment the dog approaches the card and touches it with his nose, mark and reward. For this exercise, you can introduce the verbal cue for the desired behaviour ('touch') straightaway as either the dog aims for the card, or not – in which case you would not be marking his behaviour.

You can progress by adding duration to the touch, which can be used as a calming device, helping the dog to slow down:

- When the dog touches the card, don't mark straightaway. The dog will then offer a second touch. Mark this one and, from this point, only mark and reward firm touches, when the dog exerts more pressure when he touches the card. Ignore softer touches and the dog will try again with a firmer touch, which you can mark and reward.
- We don't need duration just yet, just pressure. He is now learning to push. If you keep your hand still, he will learn to push against it, which is the start of building duration.
- Once you have that pressure, you can start marking and rewarding for duration of pressure. This should be built slowly, a second at a time. Try not to push the card against the dog's nose. Let him apply pressure, not you.

3. PUSH

Objective: Using a nose touch to push an item until it either moves or falls over.

You will need: Treats, cardboard kitchen roll insert, paper cups. I recommend using the kitchen roll insert (or toilet roll insert) as they are not only cheap but also lightweight. This means they will not make a noise when they tumble down, which could startle the dog and affect performance going forward.

Verbal cues:-
'Wait' – to ask the dog to wait on his base.
'Watch' – so the dog can observe the set-up, prior to being asked to do a behaviour associated with it. This cue is most often used when the dog is in his anchor position.
'Go' – initially used for action.
'Push' – the cue for desired behaviour.

Step-by-step

- Ask the dog to sit and wait on his base so that he can watch you put a treat on the floor and then place a cardboard insert over the top of it. It is important that you put the treat on the floor and cover it with the insert. If you drop the treat into the insert, the dog is likely to snuffle around the top of it, and it will not fall over cleanly. Going forward, when there are more inserts, we want them to fall over into each other, which means they need to be pushed from the base.

Choose lightweight objects to teach the 'push' behaviour.

- Invite the dog to come forward, using your action cue. Because he has watched you put the treat on the floor and then cover it, he will go directly to the cardboard insert and sniff the bottom of it. As the insert is light in weight, all the dog needs to do is give it a gentle push with his nose and it will roll out of the way, revealing the treat. This gives the dog an instant reward, but I also like to celebrate with him, with a clap of my hands or verbal praise. This keeps the session fun and positive, triggering the release of serotonin which will have a beneficial effect on the dog's state of mind, as well as assisting with learning and memory.
- Repeat a couple of times to build up some short-term memory. Each time, make sure you ask the dog to return to his anchor position so that he can watch you set up the exercise.
- When the dog is achieving a success rate that is clearly above average, replace the action cue with the cue for the desired behaviour – 'push'.

Ideally you should always try to move towards tertiary reinforcers, which is when performing the task becomes a reward in itself. Obviously, this can only happen when learning is fully established and the dog can perform the behaviour consistently on cue. In order to change the dog's perception so the behaviour/ task is the reward, you need to make sure he is having the best time. Therefore, use a high rate of reinforcement to start with to get the happy hormones flowing, and make yourself fun when you are giving the treats. In this way you are becoming part of the reinforcement history, which means you will not need the high rate of food rewards going forward. You should also introduce other rewards that your dog values, such as play and movement. So instead of giving a treat as a reward, mark him and then play with him. The dog understands that it was the behaviour/task that triggered the fun, so he starts to enjoy performing the behaviour in its own right.

4. LOOK

Objective: No action required – the dog simply needs to look at whatever it is you are showing him.

You will need: Treats, a piece of thick card.

Verbal cues:-
'Wait' – so the dog stays on his base.
'Good' – verbal marker (or clicker if you are using one).
'Look' – the cue for the desired behaviour.

Here you can see the dog responding to his 'look' cue so that he focuses on the item he is being shown.

Step-by-step
- Ask your dog to go to his base. This is a good place to start because the dog already knows that he must stay in position and watch what you are doing.
- Hold a piece of card behind your back, out of sight from the dog. Then quickly produce it in his eyeline. As soon as he looks at it, mark him.
- Return to your dog's base and reward him there. If he comes towards you, take him

back to his base and place a treat on it. In this way he will learn that the treat is only served on his base, which will encourage him to be close to the point of delivery.
- Repeat several times to establish a pattern of what will be reinforced and what will not. So, if he looks at you, do not mark. He needs to focus on the piece of card – not on you.

TRAINING TIP
When you are waiting for your dog to respond to a cue, do not look at him while he is in the process of thinking, otherwise he will just look at you, waiting for a clue or further instructions. Instead, look at whatever it is you want him to do. If you want him to touch a piece of paper, look at the paper. If it is something you want him to push, look at that item.

This will help to maintain his interest/ focus on what he should be doing. If your eyes are on him, he will stop trying to work out what to do and switch to waiting mode – waiting for you to help him out by giving him another cue, or showing him what to do. He will learn to wait for you to help him instead of learning to work it out all by himself, which will, in fact, give him a great deal of satisfaction.

- Change things up a bit by producing the card from your left, from your right, and at different heights, and mark the dog looking at it.
- At this stage, he will be looking at the card for an instant and will then look at you for his marker. However, if this exercise is to be useful, we need to add duration. To do this, stay silent as you present the card, and then jiggle it up and down. The movement will keep his focus on the card, allowing you to mark and reward after a slightly longer interval. This can be built up incrementally. Build slowly, adding the verbal cue, 'look' when he is focusing on the card for a couple of seconds. Progress to a maximum of 4 seconds, which ensures the dog has had a really good chance to look at the card.

We have now trained the four basic behaviours that the dog can use to indicate his choice. He now needs to learn the 'show me' cue so that he knows when you want him to make his choice.

SHOW ME
Objective: The dog indicates his choice. Typically, you would make use of this after showing him a sample item and then asking him to indicate a corresponding item.
You will need: Treats, a thick piece of card, masking tape/Blu Tac.
Verbal cues:-
'Wait' – so the dog stays on his base.
'Good' – verbal marker (or clicker if you are using one).
'Show me' – tells him to go to the wall, for example, make a decision and then indicate his choice to you.

This behaviour - where the dog indicates his choice - is used extensively in games designed to showcase cognitive skills.

Step-by-step

- For this exercise, you need a wall/barrier which has a minimum width of 2m. You will need to stand between the wall and the dog, i.e., the wall on your left, the dog on your right, or vice versa.
- Ask the dog to go to his base. Position yourself at a distance of a metre or so from him and hold a piece of card behind your back.

Note: If the wall is on your left, hold the card in your *right* hand so you can use your left hand to send the dog to the wall. If the wall is on your right, hold the card in your *left* hand so that you can send the dog to the wall using your right hand.

- Assuming that the wall is on your left, produce the card in your right hand and, using your left arm, make a sweeping gesture towards the wall. Always use the arm nearest to the wall, as it makes the signal easier to follow. When your arm is at full stretch, say "show me" In this instance, you will be using the cue before the dog has fully learnt the behaviour because your arm signal is indicating the direction he should take.
- Stand still and make sure you look at the card (or the item you want your dog to go to), rather than the dog. Wait quietly, giving him the opportunity to think about what he should be doing next. The chances are he will try something that has previously been successful and has earnt him reinforcement. Make sure you don't hold your hand too low or the dog may interpret this as the signal for a hand touch, whereas you want him to touch the card you are holding in your hand.
- You are waiting for your dog to go towards the card and touch it – then you can mark and reward. The dog can show his choice with a nose touch, or indicate with his paw if the item is at a low level.
- Allow him to choose. The object of the exercise is for the dog to make a decision and indicate his choice, so the manner in which he performs the behaviour is irrelevant. Repeat this step several times to fully establish the behaviour before moving on.
- The next step is to move the card gradually towards the wall. The goal is to hold the card against the wall and then cue "show me". When the dog is confidently targeting the card as it is held against the wall, rather than in your hand, you are ready to progress.
- Using an appropriate adhesive, stick the card to the wall, and repeat the exercise, using your outstretched arm to indicate the wall, along with your verbal cue, "show me".
- After a few trials, you should be able to stand a little further from the wall and send the dog to touch the card from a distance of a metre, or so.
- The next step is to stand on either side of the wall so the dog does not become preoccupied with your position. Build this up slowly, starting with just a step or so away from the wall, so the dog learns to target the card regardless of where you are standing (on the left or on the right), or how far you are from the wall.

Note: Imagine you are running up to a wall and putting your nose on a target time after time. It may well start to feel uncomfortable. It is just the same for your dog. So, if he starts to indicate the card using the side of the head instead of his nose, I would still accept it. It may not be the precise indication you were asking for, but it is clear that the dog is still making an informed choice.

Chapter Five
LET THE GAMES COMMENCE!

I believe in getting off to a good start, and if this is the first time you and your dog have tried skills training, it makes sense to make things easy and achievable. If you attempt one of the more difficult games in the early stages, it is likely to be a frustrating experience for both of you.

Teaching an 'easy' skill, i.e., one that is lower in criteria, is great for novice handlers, dogs under eight months of age, and dogs who are post-surgery, or recovering from injury. Easy games are also a great option if the weather is lousy or you have a little time to kill and fancy a bit of fun.

BASIC SET-UP
All you need is:
- Bed/mat/platform to use as your dog's base.
- Pre-stuffed kong.
- Cut up treats.
- Fresh drinking water for your dog.

ADDITIONAL EQUIPMENT
This will be referenced in the step-by-step instructions for each game. It includes:
- Hand towel.
- Tea towel.
- Paper cups.
- Toy.

A bed or a similar anchor point (see *page 41*), gives your dog an ideal base from which he can sit and watch you set up the exercise. The base also gives the dog a place to rest at intervals during the training session and he will learn to go there voluntarily. Brain games are very tiring so avoid lengthy sessions, and too many repetitions. Remember the ten-treat training rule (see *page 36*).

AUDIO DISCRIMINATION
Objective: We are going to train the dog to stay in position while you say a string of words. He must ignore these and respond only when he hears his release cue, i.e., a verbal cue that tells him he can stop doing the behaviour you have asked for. He is thus learning to discriminate between words that have no meaning for him and a cue that tells him he can change his behaviour.

You will need: Treats.

Verbal cues:-

'Sit' or 'down' (whichever your dog prefers when asked to stay).

'Stay'.

'OK'– a release cue to end the behaviour. The choice of word is up to you; it could be 'break', 'free',' release', etc., If your dog does not have a release cue, but has a stay, he will learn a release cue from the following exercise.

The set-up position – you can choose a 'sit' or a 'down' depending on the dog's personal preference.

Step-by-step

If your dog already knows 'stay', i.e.,' stay on that spot and do not move until I return to you', this game will be easy!

- Send the dog to his base and ask for a 'sit' (or a 'down'). Now ask him to stay, using a hand signal – flat palm – along with a verbal cue. Don't position your hand directly in front of the dog's face as this could look like an invitation to get up and interact. You also need to make sure that he can see your face, which means you can also see him. If you cannot see each other, the dog may be tempted to get up so that he is able to see your face, which is counter-productive to what you are trying to achieve.
- While the dog is in the 'stay' position, maintain your hand signal and remain on the spot. Initially, the aim is to make this exercise as easy as possible, so there is no need to add your movement or increase distance at this stage. Keeping it simple will ensure the dog focuses on learning his release cue and will remove/minimise the possibility of errors.
- Now choose three words that bear no resemblance to your 'stay' cue, or the word you are going to use for your release cue. I suggest using colours, for example, 'orange', 'pink', 'yellow' or holiday destinations, 'Barbados', 'Spain', 'Greece'. Choose anything you like – just make sure it sounds nothing like your release cue, not even starting with the same syllable.
- Say your three words out loud, accompanied by your 'stay' hand signal, which needs to be clearly visible to the dog.
- Now say your release cue, for example, "OK", and stop giving the stay hand signal. As you say your release cue, move a short distance from the dog and allow him to come to you for his reward and eat it from your hand.
- Practise a few more times so the dog learns to discriminate between non-release cue words when he stays in place, and the release cue when he goes to get his reward.
- At a later stage you can increase criteria – for example, working from a distance – but don't be in too much of a hurry. Learning the cue, and listening intently at a short distance, is the primary objective.

TRAINING TIP

It is important that you don't use a tone of voice that excites your dog during this exercise, as it might encourage him to break his stay. A calm approach is more likely to produce a successful outcome. You may want to change the tone of your voice for the non-release cue, but the release cue should always sound the same. I suggest using a higher tone of voice, indicating a slight increase in excitement, so that your dog learns to recognise – and love – his release cue!

ROLL AND REVEAL

Objective: This exercise involves the dog pushing a rolled-up towel with his nose, to reveal treats that have been concealed within the towel.

You will need: Treats, a hand towel.

Verbal cues:-

'Wait' – to ask the dog to wait and watch as you set up the exercise.

'OK' – release cue.

'Push' – You can use this cue for the action of rolling out the towel but, to be honest, once your dog has watched you cover the treats and roll up the towel, he will know exactly what to do and will get to work as soon as you give his release cue.

Canine Cognitive Skills

Keep the treats in the middle, and close together, as you roll up the towel.

Use the verbal cue, "push", and this will prompt the dog to unroll the towel and reveal the treats.

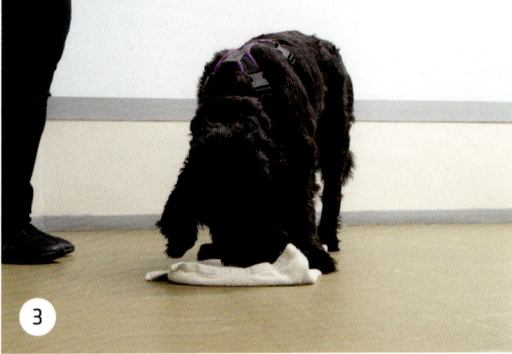

You can have a jackpot of treats at the end of the towel.

Step-by-step

- Ask the dog to go to his base and wait so he can watch you roll up the treats in the towel.

Rolling the towel involves a number of stages:

- Place treats in the middle area of the towel, and the then fold it. It is important to place the treats in the middle of the towel as it encourages the dog to push straight down the middle to reveal the treats. If you place the treats ad-hoc, he will unroll the towel in a haphazard fashion rather than in a straight line.
- Place more treats in the middle of towel and fold it again. Continue doing this, placing treats every few centimetres or so, and then roll again. Placing treats fairly close together makes it easier and therefore more exciting and profitable for the dog, which means he will really want to do it.
- Stop rolling the towel when there is approximately 30cm to spare. This is for the dog to stand on as he unrolls the towel. His weight acts as a ballast, allowing him to roll the towel away from him without it getting snarled up.
- For each trial/rep place several treats at the very end of the towel, so that when the dog has finished unrolling it, he finds a pot of gold – a jackpot of treats waiting for him.
- Initially, roll the towel fairly tight, as this makes it easier for the dog to unroll. When he becomes more experienced, you can roll it more loosely to increase the challenge.
- When you are ready, call your dog from his base. Use the verbal cue, 'push', which means he must push with his nose. This is all he needs to do to start unrolling the towel. When the treats are revealed, he will be quick to get the idea and will continue unrolling until he reaches his jackpot of treats at the end.

TRAINING TIP
If the dog is using his paws, rather than his nose, use more treats in the towel and place them closer together so he can smell them.

- When learning is fully established, slowly reduce the number of treats over time until the dog has to unroll the entire towel before reaching his jackpot.

FIND MY FACE!
Objective: This is a wonderful way to encourage your dog not only to give you eye contact but also to turn it the other way round so the dog is asking you to reciprocate.
You will need: Treats.
Verbal cues:-
'Good' – verbal marker (or clicker if you are using one).
'Face' – cues the dog to look at your face. However, in the initial stages, I use a marker – 'good' – to encourage the dog to focus on me, and maintain his focus. Your dog will learn to love his marker word as it tells him he are doing the right thing – and reinforcement is on its way.

Be quick to mark the behaviour – giving eye contact – so you can reinforce it.

Step-by-step
- Ask your dog to sit, which means he will automatically be looking at you. This means you can start with a high rate of reinforcement (see *page 28*) because the dog is already showing the desired behaviour. Mark him as soon as he looks at your face and reward.

TRAINING TIP
Keep the treats in a bowl nearby and select one each time your dog shows the desired behaviour. If you hold the treats in your hands – and move your fingers, playing with the treats – the dog will watch your hands and will not look up at your face. If, for some reason, you need to hold the treats, put your hands behind your back.

- When you establish eye contact, click if you are using a clicker or use a verbal marker and reward each time the dog looks up at your face. It is important to reward by dropping the treats on the floor so that he switches focus away from your face to the floor. This means he will choose to look up at your face after eating the treats, which sets him up for success. After a few reps, a pattern is established and his default behaviour will be to look back to your face as soon as he has eaten the treat.
- Now take a few steps away from your dog, still facing him. Call him to you, but instead of looking at the dog, look at the floor in front of you, focusing on the spot where you want him to be. Wait patiently and, because you are looking at the floor in front of you, he will arrive in that position and look up at your face.
- When the dog appears in your eye-line, mark and reward, throwing the treat on the floor. If he takes his time to arrive,

Canine Cognitive Skills

speak to him but keep looking at the floor in front of you. It does not really matter what you say, but as you speak your dog will approach to find out what is going on.
- Repeat for a few trials. When he is quick to appear in your eye-line after getting his treat, repeat, but this time stand side on to the dog so that he has to move to the front to look at your face.
- After a few more reps, walk away from the dog and stand still with your back to him. Wait for him to arrive in front of you so that he is able to see your face. As soon as he seeks eye contact, mark and reward!

IGNORING VISUAL DISTRACTIONS

Objective: Teaching the dog to ignore his peripheral vision. This means the dog has to concentrate on what is in his direct line of sight and ignore distractions which are visible on either side.

You will need: Treats, plus a toy or a knotted tea towel. I recommend using a small toy that fits easily in your hand, such as a small tug toy, a ball on a rope, or a small stuffed toy. However, if a toy is too exciting for your dog (see *page 23*), I would use a knotted tea towel, which, again, I can hold in one hand.

Verbal cues:-

'Watch' – cues the dog to look at you. Personally, I don't use a verbal cue for this behaviour. I use the dog's name to get attention, which means he is looking at me, and listening to me, and then reward.

Step-by-step

- Start with the dog sitting in front of you and hide the toy behind your back. Hold the toy in either your left hand, or your right hand, and stick to this for the initial stages of learning. This will make it easier because you are not swapping hands, and it also makes it simpler for the dog. If you

Start by hiding a toy behind your back.

Now produce it – and wait for the dog to switch focus back to your face.

are producing the toy from both your left hand and your right hand, he may become preoccupied with this aspect of the exercise instead of focusing on the desired goal – ignoring the toy and looking at you.
- Without warning, move the toy from behind your back and out to the side. Wiggle by rotating your wrist. Make sure you keep it moving, but don't hold it too low. You don't want the dog to interact with the toy, he just needs to observe it.
- The aim is for the dog to look away from the toy to focus on your face. When he does – because nothing else is happening – mark, and reward with your other hand. It is important to use a different reward for this, so a food reward is the obvious choice.

- Hide the toy behind your back again, and then produce it. Keep wiggling it, but say nothing. The silence motivates the dog to keep trying to work out what to do next. If you talk, the dog stops thinking about what he is doing and starts thinking about what you are doing and what you are saying. It's a distraction which can affect the dog's confidence in being able to problem-solve and complete the task. In contrast, keeping quiet allows him to think for himself. The moment you get the desired behaviour – the dog switches focus and looks at you – mark and reward.
- Keep repeating, each time extending the duration, i.e., the dog has to focus on you for longer (while you wiggle the toy), before you mark and reward.
- Repeat the entire process, but now produce the toy, using your other hand.
- Once learning is established you can up the challenge by speeding up and increasing the movement of the toy so it is even more of a distraction. Remember, once you have started wiggling the toy, you need to keep it moving otherwise the dog may think you are introducing a new element to the game and try to interact with it.
- With practice, the dog will learn to ignore the toy – no matter how much you move it, and no matter if you wiggle it by your side, at waist height, or higher – he will still focus exclusively on your face.
- If you want to increase criteria, move the toy in large circles, instead of rotating your wrist.

CATCHY, CATCHY MONKEY!

Objective: Teaching distance perception, i.e., the dog has to work out the distance between his mouth and the treat, so that he opens his mouth to catch it at the right moment. We have all laughed at dogs for messing up what we perceive as easy catches. This is not because he is being 'stupid'; it is a skill he has to learn and then perfect.

You will need: Treats.

Verbal cues:-

'Sit' – to set up the exercise.

'Watch' – to get ready for the catch.

'Catch!' – cue for the desired behaviour. You can use this verbal cue but, to be honest, the dog will do it instinctively. You could be pedantic and argue that 'catch' is not the right cue because the treat is being consumed, and when you ask your dog to 'catch' a ball, he does not eat it!

Catching a treat from a height is a learnt skill, so you will need to help the dog by holding the treat directly above his head.

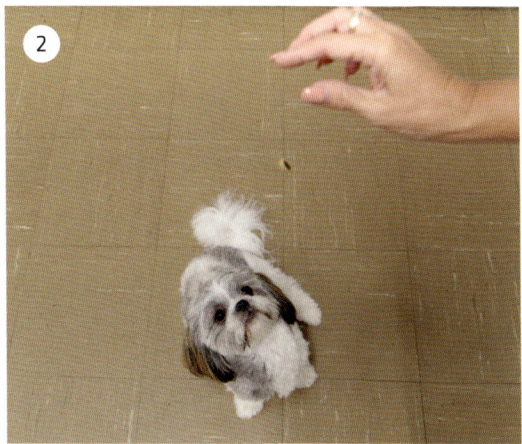

Make sure the dog keeps sitting as you drop the treat – and he will get an instant reward!

Step-by-step

- Ask the dog to sit and, holding a treat in your fingertips, position it so that it is directly above the dog's head. You want him to look up at it, but remain in the 'sit'. If he tries to jump up towards the treat, lift it higher and ask him to sit again.
- Now let the treat drop, opening your fingers wide. Your dog might catch it, or he might not. If he does catch it, praise him and repeat the exercise.
- If your dog fails to catch the treat, follow these steps:
  — As before, hold the treat above your dog's head so that he is looking up at it but, this time, hold it close to his mouth.
  — As soon as he opens his mouth, drop the treat into it.
  — Praise the dog and try several reps, keeping the treat close to his mouth.
  — Now hold the treat a couple of centimetres above his mouth and then drop it. If he does not open his mouth, wait until he does and then drop the treat into it. Praise the dog and repeat a few more times.
  — If the dropped treat is going straight into the dog's mouth, gradually increase the distance from his mouth, ensuring he is looking up at the treat.
- When the dog is catching the treat, even when you are dropping it from a height of over 1m, increase the height by a few centimetres, and see whether he catches it straightaway. The chances are he will not, because he has to adjust his perception of the height in order to catch it. Keep practising so the dog learns this skill and attains a good success rate.
- When the dog is consistently catching the treat at an increased height, you can start to vary the height of your hand so he has to make split second adjustments – timing how long it takes the treat to drop and, therefore, when to open his mouth.

COVER UP

Objective: An easy problem-solving exercise where the dog knows a treat is under the tea towel and must work out how to get it.

What you need: Treats, a tea towel.

Verbal cues:-

'Wait' – to ask the dog to wait and watch as you set up the exercise.

'Find it' – to set the dog to work to find the treat.

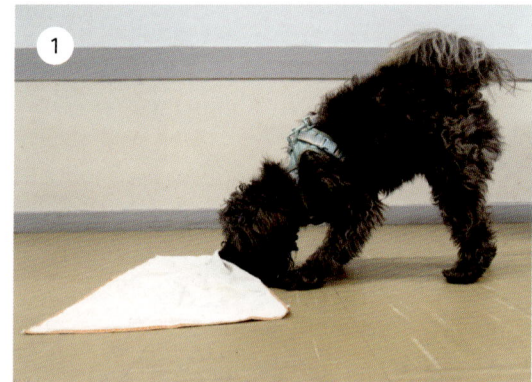

The aim is for the dog to use his nose to find the treat, so hide it near the edge of the tea towel.

Success!

Step-by-step

- Ask the dog to sit wait on his base. Holding a treat in your hand, allow him to see/sniff it.
- Making sure the dog is watching you from his anchor position, place a treat on the floor

at a distance of approximately 1m from him and cover it with a tea towel.

TRAINING TIP

The treat should not be concealed too far underneath the tea towel. This would encourage the dog to dig with his paws. It should be on the side closest to the dog so that he uses his nose to locate the treat rather than attempting to bite through the tea towel.

- Return to the dog and encourage him to find the treat under the towel, using your verbal cue, 'find it'. The aim is for the dog to work out how to get the treat, without your help. He may pick up the tea towel in his mouth, or push it back with his nose. Only give additional encouragement – moving the towel to make it easier – if the dog has been trying but is unable to access the treat. In this instance, if he looks at you for help, push back the edge of the towel so he can see the treat.
- Set up the game as before, but this time place the treat a little further under the tea towel. With practice, the dog will learn to pick up the tea towel, or push it back with his nose in order to get to the treat.

PUSH OVER

Objective: The dog uses his nose to push over a tower of paper cups. Over time, this will have the added benefit of reducing sensitivity to loud noises as the dog will be involved in a rewarding activity in the midst of tumbling cups, which will make quite a clatter, particularly as it is happening so close to his ears.

You will need: Treats, paper cups.

Verbal cues:-

'Wait' – to ask the dog to wait and watch as you set up the exercise.

'Push' – to invite the dog to push over the cups.

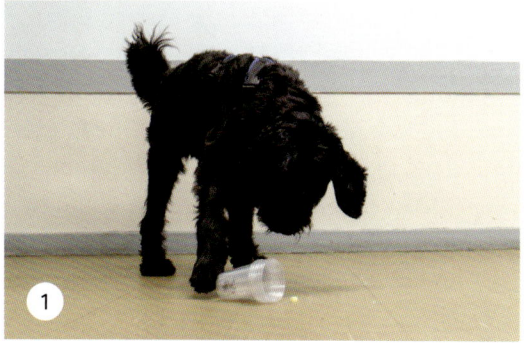

Start by placing a treat under a single cup, or stacked cups.

Give the verbal cue, "push", and the treat will be revealed.

Step-by-step

- Ask the dog to wait on his base and allow him to watch as you put a treat on the floor and then place a cup (upside down) over it. For this game, you will be working at a distance of approximately 1m from him.
- Give the verbal cue 'push'(see *page 46*), which tells the dog he must push over the cup, thereby revealing the treat. Repeat this a few times using one cup only.
- Place a second treat on the floor and cover each treat with a cup. Repeat a few times.
- Now place a row of cups side by side, with a treat under each individual cup. Repeat a few times.
- Build a small tower with two rows of upside-down cups (perhaps four on the bottom row and three on top row). The

treats are secreted under the cups in the bottom row and, in the initial stage of learning, you could also place treats on the top row. This presents a sizeable target for the dog to knock over. The increased height means it will tumble at the slightest touch, resulting in an easy 'win' and, going forward, a high ratio of success.

- When you are ready, give your verbal cue, "push". As the dog has been watching the set-up, he should need no encouragement to push the tower with his nose. As soon as the cups tumble, he will find and eat the treats. Repeat this a few times.
- When the dog is achieving a good success rate, you can increase the challenge by building a more elaborate structure. Create a bottom row by placing three cups alongside each other. The second row has two cups, and the top row has one cup, forming a triangular shape. Treats can be placed anywhere in this structure, for example, two treats under the bottom row of cups, one under the middle row, and one under the top cup.

Note: When using multiple treats, make sure they are cut up very small – approximately the size of a frozen pea.

- Now you are ready to add more cups. Each time you set up, ask the dog to wait on his base and watch you. Remember, the more cups you are using, the longer it takes to set up the game up, so you should reward him intermittently for staying in place and watching you, which will motivate him to remain in position. Keep adding more cups, one on top of one another, until you have a tower of cups.
- At this stage, confine treats to the bottom row of cups. If you continue to place treats on different rows, the dog might

Stepping up the challenge.

start to neglect the cups on the bottom row which means they will remain standing.

- When the last cup topples, have a party, praising your dog and showing him how thrilled you are. The dog will perceive this as an additional reward (on top of the treats); he will join in the fun and he will motivated to push over *all* the cups whenever he sees this sort of set-up.
- To increase the challenge, set up the cups but put do not put any treats underneath them. When the dog has pushed over the last cup, throw some treats among the fallen cups. At this stage, pushing over the cups is a tertiary reinforcer (see *page 25*) because the task itself is fun and rewarding.

This game is a great way of working on your dog's 'push' cue, i.e., learning to use his nose to push over the item you indicate. It is also a confidence booster as the dog learns that putting his head among the cups and hearing the clatter as they topple over – something that could be a cause for concern– is all part of a rewarding game.

LET THE GAMES COMMENCE!

This game is all about self-control so work in easy stages.

Speed up treat delivery when the dog fully understands what is expected of him.

WAIT FOR IT!

Objective: Teaching the dog to remain still and focused while you deliver a treat, starting in slow motion and then accelerating to a zoomie finish! This is a great game for encouraging stillness, concentration, and self-control, as well ignoring peripheral vision.

What you need: Treats.

Verbal cues:-

'Sit' – to start the exercise.
'Wait' – prior to delivering the treat.

Step-by-step

- Ask the dog to sit so that he is in a comfortable position for looking up and monitoring the treat. Now stand in front of him, with your arm outstretched, and hold a treat in your fingertips, positioned directly above his head. Make a mental note of this set-up, particularly the height of your hand, as you need to adhere to it during the initial stages of learning.
- Start by moving your treat hand very slowly towards the dog's mouth. When you have covered approximately a quarter of the distance to his mouth, speed up and zoom it down to the dog's mouth. It is important that he doesn't jump up before he gets the treat.

TRAINING TIP

If your dog jumps towards the treat move your hand back to the starting position, as quickly as you can, and wait for the dog to sit. Then start again. He will soon learn that if he jumps, you will move the treat away. As he wants you to bring it closer, he will learn to keep his bottom on the floor.

- Repeat the above step a few more times so the dog understands what is required and is showing a good level of self-control.
- Now you can gradually increase the slow section of the treat's journey to your dog's mouth to the halfway point, and then speed up for the second half. In this way, you are increasing the length of time it takes for the treat to arrive at the dog's mouth.
- The aim is for the dog to be patient and to learn to control himself. He is excited and full of anticipation because he knows the treat is going to arrive, but he must exert self-control if he is to get it.
- Working incrementally, extend the distance, and therefore the duration of the

slow-motion section so the dog has to work a little harder each time. Remember, he must remain completely still until the treat is dropped into his mouth.
- With practice, the slow portion of the journey will be longer than the fast section until you are able to deliver the treat in slow motion, from start to finish, with your dog sitting, waiting patiently for the treat to drop into his mouth. To increase the challenge, you can vary the height of your outstretched arm so the dog has to work out when the treat is going to be dropped into his mouth.

SWITCHING FOCUS

Objective: This teaches eye contact as a default behaviour. The dog learns he will be rewarded if he looks away from what he wants, i.e., the treat in your outstretched hand and, instead, looks at your face. In other words, good things happens when he looks at you!

Note: When playing Find My Face (*page 53*), the dog learns to find your face, even when you are not directly facing him. In this game, you are asking him to switch focus from a desired object so your face must be easy to access.

What you need: Treats.

Verbal cues:-

No cue initially, but once the dog starts performing the behaviour, i.e., switching focus to look at your face, you can use a cue such as 'face'.

Step-by-step

- Ask the dog to sit, and face him. With a treat in your hand (you can choose either left or right), extend your arm fully at a 90-degree angle from the side of your body. You can either stand or sit for this exercise; I prefer to sit so the dog does not have to stretch his neck to look at me. However, if the dog tries to jump up, you will need to stand so that your hand is out of reach.
- From his sitting position, the dog will watch as you move your arm, as he is focusing on the treat in your hand. Now keep your hand very still; say and do nothing, but keep a close eye on your dog. Eventually, because nothing is happening, he will look at you for

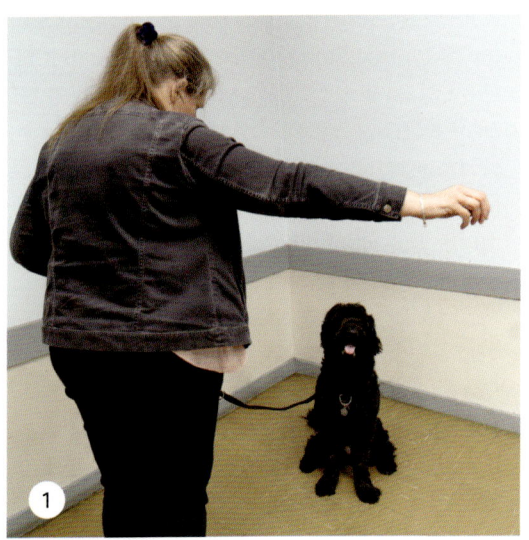
The dog is focused on the treat in the handler's hand.

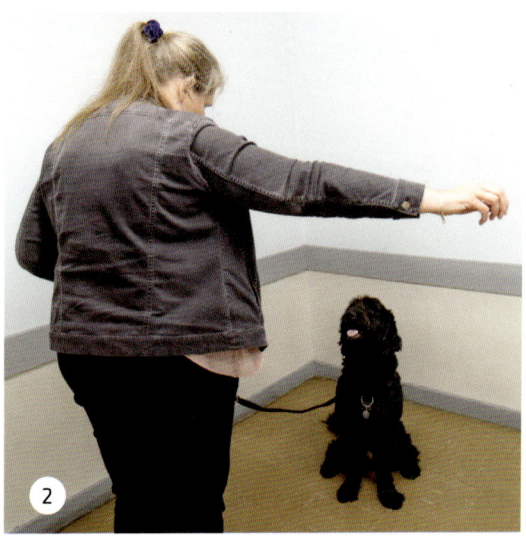
Now he has switched focus to the handler's face.

- direction on what to do next.
- As soon as the dog looks away from the treat and looks at your face – this might be a head turn or just the flick of an eye – mark and give him the treat immediately.
- Don't communicate with the dog, apart from marking the correct 'look at my face' behaviour. That is the point when the dog has to work it out and problem-solve.
- Repeat the exercise with another treat, again holding it in your outstretched arm at 90 degrees from your body. Continue with several more reps, so the dog learns that he will be rewarded if he looks at your face rather than the treat.
- When your dog is achieving a good success ratio, i.e., for the majority of reps he is choosing to look at your face rather than the treat, you can start to increase criteria and make it a little harder. To start with, swap hands. So, if you have been holding the treat in your left hand, now hold it in your right (or vice versa) so the treat is being presented on the other side of your body. Work on this for a few reps, and then mix it up, swapping between the two sides of your body. You can also try holding the treat at different heights – and even above your head.
- Now let's increase the criteria even further! As before, hold a treat in your hand at 90 degrees to the side of your body, but this time you are going to introduce movement. Rotate your wrist and keep it moving. Do not stop and start, otherwise the dog will become preoccupied with the change in movement. Wait for him to look away from your moving hand and at your face, and then mark and give him the treat. Repeat until the dog understands what is required.
- When he is coping with movement from your wrist, step it up and use your elbow to create circular movements. As before, maintain the movement until the dog looks away from the treat to look at your face. Mark and give him the treat. Repeat to establish learning.
- Next, you can move your arm in a circular movement from the shoulder, creating a major distraction. Again, mark and reward the dog for ignoring this and looking at your face. You can then repeat all stages of movement – wrist, elbow, shoulder – and practise on both sides of your body.

Chapter Six
INCREASING THE CHALLENGE

Once you and your dog have mastered the games for beginners, you are ready to progress to the next level. By now your dog has acquired some key skills, and you may well find that he is paying you a lot more attention.

Stepping up the challenge involves increasing criteria, which means giving fewer hints to the dog so he has to think a little harder about what he should be doing.

These games are great for dogs aged eight months and older, who have developed sufficient brain maturity and, in particular, brain plasticity, to compute the information received from internal and external stimuli.

Brain plasticity, which applies equally to human brains, has a big impact on the ability to learn. When a dog learns something new, his brain maps the information. If we go on to make changes or add more layers of learning, the brain remaps itself to adapt to the new information. This skill will be employed throughout a dog's lifetime, but it will deteriorate in older age.

Early learning should always take place inside as the external environment has too many distractions in terms of what the dog can see, smell, and hear.

Therefore, I recommend playing these games on those days when it is raining and no one wants to go out, or when you have run out of time for a long walk. A shorter walk, followed by a 20-minute session of cognitive games, will give your dog a real workout.

BASIC SET-UP
As before, you will need basic set-up equipment, which includes:
- A bed/crate/platform to use as your dog's base.
- A pre-stuffed kong.
- Cut up treats, both low and high value (see *page 40*).
- Fresh drinking water for your dog.

ADDITIONAL EQUIPMENT
Additional equipment will be referenced in the step-by-step instructions for each game. It includes:
- Your dog's food bowl.
- Two coloured bowls.
- Car keys.
- Clear plastic lid.
- Cake tray.
- Scent pods (see *page 72*).
- Shoe box.
- Thick piece of card
- Flannel.
- Masking tape/Blu Tac
- Six tennis balls.
- Toy.
- Two A4 prints depicting 'O'.
- Two A4 prints depicting 'X'.
- Two prints featuring the same image, one big, one small.

FIND MY KEYS
Objective: Finding and retrieving a bunch of keys.
What you need: A toy or a flannel, car keys or a small bunch of keys.
Verbal cues:- 'Wait', 'Watch', 'Find it', Find my keys'.

Your dog may find the taste of metal a little off-putting, and he may also

INCREASING THE CHALLENGE

find a keyring with a number of keys a little too heavy in the early stages of learning. Therefore, to start the exercise, I recommend using something small – perhaps a small toy – which the dog is happy to hold in his mouth. I find that a soft flannel, tied in a knot so it is easy to pick up, also works well.

When I introduce the keyring, I select a couple of keys and put them on a keyring so it is not too weighty. I then attach the toy or flannel so that the dog can seek it out by scent. In the following instructions, I will use a toy as an example.

Step-by-step

- Regardless of whether you are using a toy or a flannel, you want your dog to regard it as being special. Position the dog in front of you and pique his interest by stroking the toy and talking to it so that he wants to join in. But don't give it to him straightaway!
- Continue stroking and talking to the toy and move a step or so away from your dog. Don't look at him, focus all your attention on the toy. The dog will become curious and will want what you have or, at the very least, he will want to see what it is.
- Allow the dog to approach, look directly at him and ask him if he wants the toy. A soon as he is focused on it, allow him to take hold and have a brief game of interactive tug. Make sure you don't let go of it at this stage. The anticipation, and the game, means that the toy now has value and you can use it as a reward going forward.
- Following the game of tug, ask your dog to release the toy and then ask him to sit and wait on his base. Ask him to "watch" (or make sure he is watching) as you

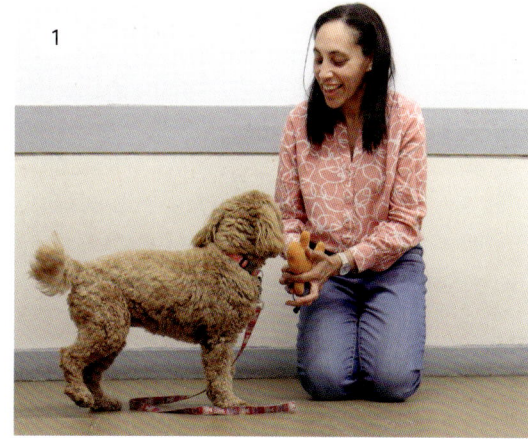

The basics of the game are taught using a flannel or a toy – the keyring is attached when learning is established. The first step is to get the dog interested in the toy.

Let the dog watch as you partly hide the toy.

Send the dog to find the toy.

Encourage him to bring it back to you.

- hide the toy in a relatively easy spot (for example, under a rug, under a sofa, or behind a bag), making sure a bit of it is poking out so he can see it.
- Return to the dog and ask him to 'find it'. When he has the toy in his mouth, stay where you are, clapping your hands and verbally praising him. Then go in and play tuggy with him, which is his reward for finding the toy. Repeat this step several times. Bear in mind, this is not a game of hide-and-seek, so the dog should watch you hiding the toy. He will then go directly to find it, and you can celebrate with a game of tug.
- Now hide the toy in the same place but, this time, make sure it is completely concealed with no part sticking out. Ask the dog to 'find it' and reward with a game of tug. Repeat several times.
- The next step is to hide the toy in a different place, making use of different piece of furniture, or a rug in a different location. As we have made it more difficult, go back to leaving part of the toy visible.
- When your dog has got the idea of going to a different place, keep changing it so he finds the toy in two or three different locations. If he is coping with this and, hopefully, going to the correct place at the first time of asking, you are ready to move to the next step.
- Now you can conceal the toy – with no part showing – still allowing the dog to watch you place it. This allows him to be successful, which will keep him motivated. This is important when he has to try harder, searching with his nose rather than his eyes.
- The dog has now mastered the basics so you are ready to attach your keyring to the toy and continue to hide it, adding a cue of 'find my keys!'. Because you have played this game, the dog will learn to sniff out your keys and he will be able to retrieve them as the toy is attached.
- To increase criteria, you could make sure the dog is not watching when you hide the keys and then ask him to find them. However, I would help him to be successful by indicating the area he should search.

TEACHING A RETRIEVE

Ideally, you want the dog to bring the keys to you when he is working over a greater distance. Some dogs will naturally retrieve a toy, and this can be encouraged when you are playing tuggy. However, I also make use of food. This is what I do:

- When I send the dog out to find an item, I wait until he has picked it up and then I move towards his base.
- I clap my hands – which means the dog is not aware that I have a treat – and use lots of verbal encouragement so he comes towards me. You can also use your recall cue, 'come' so he understands he must come to you.
- I delay putting treat on the base until the dog arrives, otherwise he may be tempted to drop the item before he gets to his base. Instead, I put the treats down as he comes into me. I take the item from the dog's mouth, allowing him to enjoy an instant reward – eating treats from his base. When learning is established you can, if you wish, introduce a specific cue, such as 'fetch'.

INCREASING THE CHALLENGE

- Once the behaviour is strong enough, you can transfer the game outside, starting in the garden and progressing to the park or a field if he is stepping up to the challenge.

TIDY UP!

Objective: Dropping items in a box/basket.
What you need: Treats, shoe box or basket, items such as toys that are easy to pick up and will fit inside the box.
Verbal cues:-
'Get it' – to pick up a toy.
'Come/fetch' – to bring the toy to you.
'Drop' – to drop the toy into the box/basket.
'Wait' – if you are adding distance.
'Tidy' – to cue the game.

This is a great game and comes in very handy if you have a dog who likes to steal items around the house. Instead of chasing your dog round the kitchen table to retrieve his 'trophy', you can simply ask him to drop it in a box. Regardless of this practical application, it is simply a fun game to play with your dog.

Step-by-step

- Place the basket on the floor in front of you and kneel behind it. Now position a toy on the floor directly in front of the basket and encourage your dog to pick it up. You can do this by touching the toy, moving it a couple of centimetres, or tossing it in the air and telling the dog to 'get it'.
- Gently clap your hands, and hold them together over the top of the basket. This will encourage the dog to bring the toy to your hands. At no time should you try to take the toy from the dog or attempt to touch it while he is holding it. This could have the adverse effect of making him back off, which is the total opposite of what we are trying to achieve.
- When the dog picks up the toy, maintain a

Position yourself in front of the basket so you can direct operations. Start by encouraging the dog to pick up a toy.

Hold your hand over the basket so the dog aims for them. Then give the verbal cue, "drop".

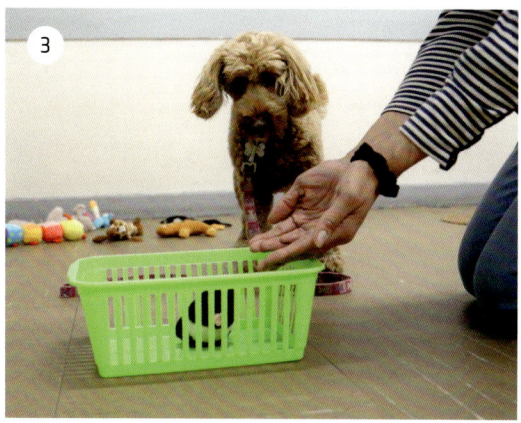

The toy lands in the basket.

65

calm tone of voice and encourage him to bring it towards you, using the dog's name, and a recall cue – 'come', or 'fetch' if he knows how to retrieve. (see Teaching a Retrieve, *page 64*).

- If you mark the dog too soon, he may drop the toy, thinking all he has to do is pick it up and drop it to get a reward. If the dog brings it close to the basket and drops it when he is less than a foot from it, place a treat in the basket, let him eat it, and then start again. In this way, the dog learns that food is only delivered in the basket. Therefore, he will head to the basket when he has the toy in his mouth and, hopefully, he will drop it over the basket to eat the treat. *Voila!* He has dropped the toy exactly where you want it.

- We can reward for whatever behaviour the dog offers, i.e., we can reward him as he gets closer to the basket, with the toy in his mouth, until he reaches our final behavioural goal dropping the toy in the basket. At this stage you can introduce a verbal cue, such as 'drop'.

- If the dog approaches the basket and drops the toy in your hands, allow it to drop from your hands and into the basket. This is your marker point, where you can use your marker word or clicker. As the toy lands, drop a treat in the basket to reward him. The treat should *always* be delivered into the basket.

- As the dog gains understanding of the task, you can toss the toy slightly further from the basket and then encourage him to bring it to the basket and drop it inside. If your dog already likes a fetch game this will be easier for you both. The key is to deliver the treat *after* he has dropped the toy in the basket. You can set him up for this exercise by introducing a 'wait' and a verbal cue, such as 'tidy'.

- To increase the challenge you can ask the dog to 'tidy' different items – a different toy, your car keys, a face flannel, a coaster – making sure they are easy to pick up, small enough to carry, and not a prized possession that the dog will want to take away to his bed to enjoy. You can then progress to setting out multiple items for the dog to 'tidy'.

PRESS THE BUTTON

Objective: A 50/50 choice game where you offer both hands and the dog has to 'press the button', i.e., respond to a hand signal, in order to get his reward. This game is a great favourite with all my students; it is always a 'go to' when they are asked to select a game that both dog and handler enjoy equally!

What you need: Treats.

Verbal cue:-
'Choose' – to choose which hand to 'press'.

Step-by-step

- Hold a tasty treat in one hand and allow your dog to smell it so that he knows it is there. Now close your hand in a fist. The other hand should be offered with a flat palm, with all fingers held tightly together, obviously without a treat.

- Position the dog in front of you and offer both hands, held close together. One is closed encasing the treat and one is flat, palm facing the dog. Initially he might sniff around the closed fist. Stay silent and keep your hand deadly still. Just wait. Eventually, he will stop sniffing your fist and start investigating the other hand.

- Wait for the dog to touch the flat hand, even if this happens by accident, and mark him instantly. At the same time, open your other hand – the one holding the treat – and allow the dog to eat it. *Do not* move the treat hand towards the dog. He must come to the hand when it is held in its original position, otherwise he will wait for the treat to be moved towards him.

- Gradually, widen the distance between your hands, so when the dog presses the button, i.e., touches the flat hand, you can mark him for a correct choice, and he then moves to your other hand to get the treat. You can also increase your own distance from the dog.
- Now swap hands, putting the treat in your other hand. This hand will now be offered as a closed fist, and the other will be presented as a flat palm. Repeat the previous steps, offering both hands close together and then gradually moving them apart. The goal is to stand with your arms fully outstretched so the dog is moving at speed, first running to your flat hand and then to your fist to get the treat.
- With practice, the dog will learn to look at both hands and then choose the flat palm. Learning how to position your hands for each trial, and remembering which hand to keep flat and which holds the treat, is easier said than done, and has been the cause of much hilarity in my workshops!

NOUGHTS AND CROSSES

Objective: The dog is cued to identify an X or an O and to indicate his choice.

What you need: Treats, food bowl, two A4 prints, one depicting an X symbol, the other depicting an O symbol, blue tac/masking tape.

Verbal cues:-
 'Look' – to focus on the print.
 'Show me' – to indicate his choice.

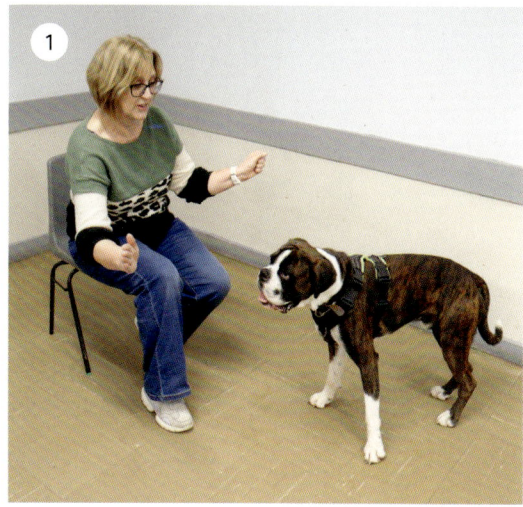

Offer both hands– but the one holding the treat is presented as a closed fist.

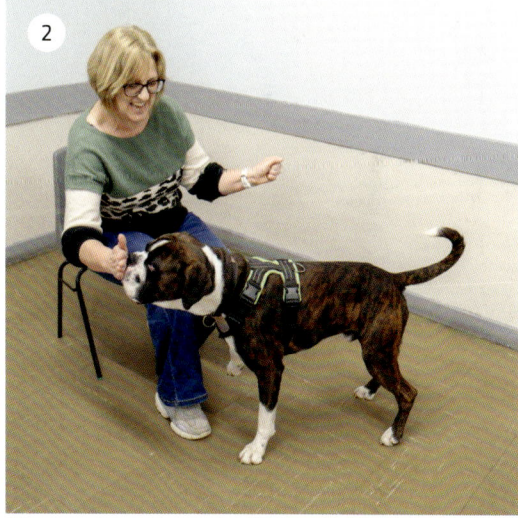

To get the treat, the dog needs to 'press the button,' i.e., touch the other hand.

SUCCESS RATIO

In this game, you are aiming for a success ratio that is 'clearly above average'. So, for example, if you did 10 trials and the dog got six or more correct, it would be counted as above average. A ratio below six that are correct, would be considered below average. So 'clearly above average' means *mostly* correct.

PLAYING NOUGHTS AND CROSSES

1

The set-up: This enables the dog to make his choice, turn and head for the treat bowl, and then be in position for the next trial. In the initial stages, work on one symbol – in this case the X – before adding the O print.

2

Show the dog the symbol you want him to choose.

3

Ask him to go and find the matching symbol.

4

Success!

INCREASING THE CHALLENGE

Step-by-step

The foundation or baseline training for this game is for the dog to choose the same symbol each time. I will use an X as an example in the following instructions:

- Place your dog's food bowl on the floor at sufficient distance from a wall so that you position yourself between the two. To start with, hold the A4 print depicting an X symbol in your hand and encourage the dog to touch it with his nose. As soon as he co-operates, toss a treat in his food bowl. The set-up for this exercise is important as it promotes fluidity of movement in the decision-making process. As we progress – and the X print is stuck on the wall – the dog will turn from the wall to go to his bowl to eat the treat, and immediately turn back to face you and the wall again, ready for the next trial.
- After a few successful trials where the dog touches the X print in your hand, start to move it towards the wall. Now the dog has to move progressively closer to the wall in order to touch the X print and earn his reward, which is, again, tossed in his bowl.
- Repeat the above, until you are holding the print against the wall and the dog is touching it in position. Continue to reward by tossing treats into the food bowl.
- The next step is to attach the X print to the wall (with Blu Tac or similar and send the dog to touch it – "show me" (see *page 48*). If the wall is on your right, produce the X print with your *left* hand and use you *right* hand to send the dog to the wall, while giving your 'show me' cue. Remember to look at the print on the wall – not the print in your hand.
- When he has touched the X, toss a treat into his bowl, which will behind him when he is touching the print on the wall. This puts him in a good position to start the next trial. Make sure you use the correct hand for presenting the print, and the other hand for sending the dog. Try to make your movement as fluid as possible as this will ensure you don't interrupt the dog's thought process and will encourage him to move smoothly from your side to the wall.
- Now, when he is returning from eating his reward, present the X print from behind your back and place it on your chest, saying 'look'. At this point, you could name the letter on the print, instead of saying "look". If you decide to do this, you will need to be consistent and name the letter each time you present it. Ideally, I want this game to be a visual exercise so I choose not to name the letter but, obviously, you can change the exercise to suit you and your dog.
- Once the dog targets the X print, mark him and reward with a treat in his bowl. Continue with this for a few trials to strengthen the behaviour, repeating until your dog is going to the 'X' fluidly.

We can now step up the criteria and introduce discrimination and choice. Remember it's a 50/50 choice game.

- Now attach the O print (non-rewarding) to the wall, leaving a minimum gap of 25cm (12in) from the X print.
- Stand in a direct line from the X print, and repeat the process of showing the dog the X print in your hand and sending him to the wall – "show me". Hopefully, he will ignore the O print as it is non-rewarding, and go directly to the X print because, historically, it has been rewarding for him and is in a direct line in front of him, i.e., the quickest route to reinforcement.

Now we are going to test what we have achieved so far, relying on the dog's historical learning and memory.

- Stand in line with the O print, show him the X print in your hand and send him to find the corresponding print. If he goes to the O print, freeze and wait to see if he tries again. The fact that you freeze and say nothing will tell him he has made a mistake. When he chooses the X – the only other choice available to him – mark and toss a treat in his bowl as usual. In this game, we ignore mistakes as it motivates the dog to think, try again and be successful.
- If the dog continues to make a mistake, stand closer to the wall and incline slightly forwards, which will help him to make the right decision. Repeat until the dog builds up a series of successes.
- After a few trials, swap the X and O positions and go back to standing on the X side, then the O side, so the dog learns to choose X (which triggers reinforcement) regardless of where you stand. At this stage, the dog is seeing X all the time and indicating X all the time. He is building a strong history of correct answers *and learning* that he should ignore the O despite seeing it. This means when we suddenly start to ask for the O, the dog has seen it and is more likely to choose it, because he has already learnt that he must match the print you are holding in your hand, regardless of where you are standing or whether the corresponding print is positioned on the left or right side of the wall.
- With practice, you can progress to standing behind the food bowl and sending the dog to the wall from this position.

THE POWER OF LATENT LEARNING

This is a process of learning that takes place in the background without formal teaching. So, when playing noughts and crosses, the dog is targeting the X and being rewarded for it, but during the course of the exercise, he sees the O positioned next to the X. This mean that when he is presented with an O, he knows where it is and has identified it during previous trials.

LITTLE AND LARGE

Objective: To discriminate between a big picture and a small picture by sight, plus a verbal cue: 'big' or 'small'.

To help the dog understand the difference between big and small, we use a different tone of voice: low tone for big; high tone for smaller (or vice versa). The change in tone highlights the difference between the two cues, and provides a 'hook', which the brain will use to attach a clue, thereby helping the dog to recall which is which.

What you need: Treats, food bowl, two A4 prints depicting the same image (but on one print it is big, and on the other it is small), masking tape/Blu Tac.

Verbal cues:-
'Big' – to name the large image.
'Small' – to name the small image.
'Show me' – to indicate his choice.

Step-by-step

- Attach the print with the big image to the wall and stand side-on, either left or right side. It does not matter which to start with, as we will be swapping over as we progress. Make sure you have treats at the ready and place the food bowl behind the dog's starting position (no more than a metre) just as you did when playing

INCREASING THE CHALLENGE

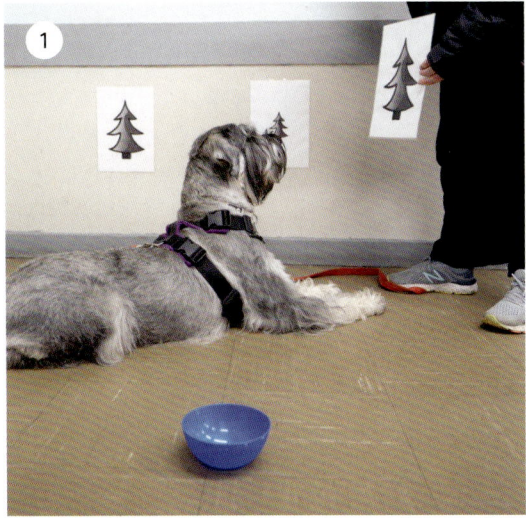

Show the dog the big image, and name it, in this case "big".

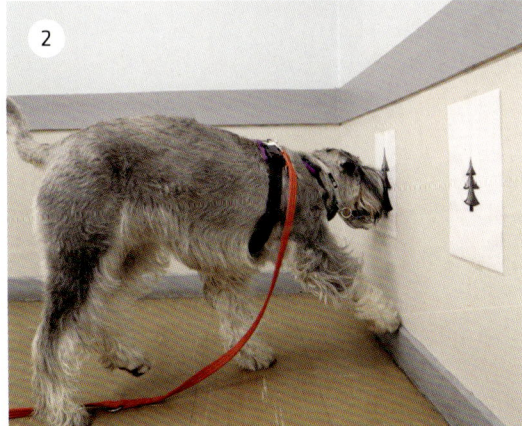

Now give your verbal cue "show me" and the dog will indicate the matching print on the wall.

- Freeze with your arm outstretched, indicating the print, until the dog goes to touch it with his nose. Remember to look at the print on the wall, not the dog; you need to look in the direction you want the dog to go. Click/mark and reward each correct touch, throwing the treat into a bowl behind the dog so that when he has eaten it, he will turn directly towards the wall, ready for the next trial.
- Repeat several times, using the verbal cues 'big' followed by 'show me' until the success ratio is a minimum of 8 out of 10. We are not looking for perfection at this stage, just clearly above average (see success ratio, *page 67*). Bear in mind the dog learns by making mistakes, so you should expect a few errors in the initial stages.
- Now stand on the opposite side of the print so that the dog is not just going left (or right) each time he hears the verbal cue, 'big'. He must learn to go to the correct print on verbal cue rather than relying on your position.
- The next step is to attach the print with the small image to the wall. This should be a minimum distance of 25cm (12in) from the print with the big image. Continue to ask for "big", initially standing on the 'big' side, i.e., the side where you started the training. At this stage, the small image is in position solely for discrimination purposes and for a little background learning: namely that as you send him to the big picture, he sees the small, but ignores it because it is non-rewarding. He will recall and use this when cued later in the exercise, making use of latent learning (see *page 70*). Mark and reward for each correct 'big' touch.
- Change sides and mark and reward for indicating 'big' when you are standing on the 'small' side.

noughts and crosses (see *page 67*). At the start of an exercise, the closer you are to the wall, the easier it is for the dog.
- By now your dog should be proficient at targeting a print attached to a wall, so ask him to nose-touch the print, saying "big", followed by "show me", using a sweeping arm gesture to indicate the big image. Make sure that you don't touch the print, as this may look as though you are asking for a hand touch.

- We are now ready to ask the dog to indicate the small image on a verbal cue. Standing on the 'small' side, ask for "small", remembering to change your tone of voice so that it completely different from the tone you used when asking for "big". Mark and reward for a correct indication by tossing a treat in the food bowl.
- If your dog indicates the big image, stand still with your arm outstretched towards the small image. Keep looking at the small image – not at the dog – and wait. When no reward or marker is forthcoming, he will try again and, ultimately, he will make the correct choice, allowing you to mark and reward. Hence, he learns from his mistakes. This should not happen too often. If the dog continues to fail, make it easier for him by standing closer to the wall. If the dog made three mistakes in a row, I suggest going back a step (dropping criteria) and progressing from this point.

WHAT IS HAPPENING?

The dog has been targeting the big image with the small image alongside. When he hears a different cue – "small" – spoken in a different tone of voice, along with your changed position, he will realise he must try something else. The small image, which he has seen, but previously ignored, is the obvious choice. Here he is tapping into latent learning, drawing on what he has learnt so far (see The power of latent learning, *page 70*).

- If the dog has gone to the incorrect image (big), stay still and silent and keep looking at the small image. Eventually, he will go to the small image and you can mark him. Remember, it is important that nothing happens if he gets it wrong so that he can learn from an incorrect choice.
- Continue cueing "big" on the 'big' side and "small" on the 'small' side, asking for the other option or on every second or third request.
- Now stand on the 'big' side and ask for "small".
- Follow this up by standing on the 'small' side and ask for "big".
- Once you have completed all of the above stages, you can stand a little further from the wall and ask the dog to target on a verbal cue, using a less exaggerated hand signal.

SHOW AND TELL

Objective: To indicate the correct scent by adopting a learnt position, for, example, a 'sit' or a 'down'.

What you need: Treats, 4-6 scent pods.

Verbal cues:-

'Sit/Down' – as the passive indicator position, i.e., the position you want the dog to adopt when he is indicating he has found the scent.

'Watch' – to observe the set-up of the exercise.

'Wait' – prior to being sent out to find the scent.

'Find it' – to find the scent.

DIY TIP

You can buy scent pods for dogs but this can be expensive. Instead, I use dome-shaped cones (used in football training) which are a better shape, with a much smaller hole in the top, so the dog cannot extract the treat.

You can also use takeaway boxes. To customise a box, you will need to create a small hole in the lid (big enough to insert a treat, but not so big the dog can extract it).

I suggest burning a hole rather than piercing the lid so that you avoid sharp edges, bearing in mind the dog will be putting his nose to the hole.

Step-by-step

The initial training involves teaching your dog a passive indicator. This is a position he will adopt when he has identified the correct scent (in this case, food) as we want him to indicate the scent – not try to get the food! The position he adopts can be either a 'sit' or a 'down', depending on the dog's natural preference. In the following instructions, I will use a 'sit'.

Note: Earmark one pod to use as your food pod and use it exclusively for this purpose. It is important that the dog cannot detect the scent of food in the other pods, as this would be highly confusing.

- First we need to make an association that the food scent equals a 'sit', which will be the default position the dog adopts when he finds the scent. This is known as a passive indicator position. Start by putting a treat into the food pod and allow your dog to sniff it while you are holding it. Make sure he doesn't eat it! When he is sniffing it, say "sit". The moment he goes into position, mark and allow him to eat the treat from the pod. Repeat this step a couple of times.
- Starting with the dog on his base, ask him to "sit" and then "wait". Stand a few paces away from the dog and, with the pod in your hand, invite him to come forward with a verbal cue – "find it" – and allow him to sniff the treat in the pod.
- When he sniffs the pod, give your verbal cue – "sit" – and mark and reward him when he does so. Repeat a few times, with the pod in your hand, to strengthen the association between sniffing the food and sitting.
- Now you are ready to put the pod on the floor. Stand a short distance from the dog, and let him watch as you put a treat through the hole in the top of the pod. Make a big show, using your cue to look, and making sure you have his full attention so he knows exactly what you have done with the treat.

Note: Do not put the treat on the floor and then put the pod on top of it, because this will result in the dog sniffing around the bottom rim of the pod instead of aiming for the hole at the top of the pod. If using a takeaway box, insert the treat through the hole you have made. Do not take off the lid to put the treat in.

- When the pod is in position, return to your dog and use a sweeping arm gesture to indicate the pod, along with your verbal cue, "find it".
- Set off with the dog so that you can arrive at the pod together, just in case he tries to help himself or play with the pod. The instant he arrives at the pod, give your verbal cue, "sit". Although we have changed the exercise slightly, the dog should draw on previous learning and make the association that the scent equals sit. Later, when there is more than one pod, he will need time to sniff and investigate but, at the moment, there is only one pod. He knows the scent is there, so we want him to use that knowledge and go into position.

TRAINING TIP

The aim is for the dog to go directly to the pod and sniff the hole at the top, rather than placing a paw on it and pushing it around in an attempt to get at the scent. If your dog attempts to nudge the pod, place your foot on it so that it will not move, and say "sit". The moment he stops touching the pod, remove your foot. If he tries to move it again, repeat the procedure, putting your foot on the pod and giving your verbal cue to sit. Remove your foot as soon as he co-operates. Try not to keep your foot on the pod any longer than necessary, otherwise the dog could make the wrong connection and think that your foot on the pod is a cue to sit.

- As soon as the dog goes into the sit position, mark and immediately lift the pod to allow him to eat the treat, keeping hold of the pod in your hand. If you are using a takeaway box, pick up the box and remove the lid to allow access to the treat. Do not place the pod back on the floor immediately after the dog has eaten the treat as he may try to play with it. Instead, keep hold of it and ask the dog to return to his starting point, i.e. his base. Repeat this step several times to strengthen the behaviour. In this way the dog will learn that if he tries to help himself, he will be denied the treat. But if he offers the sit position (which you have asked for on each trial), he will get the treat much quicker.
- Go through the whole process again but this time do not give your verbal cue to sit. Wait silently until your dog offers the behaviour. Then you can mark, pick up the pod and allow the dog to eat his reward from the floor. Be patient and be prepared to work on quite a few reps until learning is established. This will pay dividends later on as the challenge increases.
- Now you are ready to introduce a second pod, which should be placed a short distance from the first pod, in a direct line going away from the dog. A dog's natural behaviour is to go forwards, sniffing on the

The set-up.

A treat is placed in the second pod.

The dog is sent to investigate.

INCREASING THE CHALLENGE

Using his sense of smell, he locates the correct pod.

He indicates his find by adopting his default position – in this case a 'sit'.

move, so placing the pods in a line will encourage both sniffing and searching. For the first few trials, make sure the food pod is first in line. Ask the dog to "find it" and go with him as he sets off. He will arrive at the correct pod by default because it is closest to him. If he indicates, i.e., goes into a 'sit' – excellent! Mark and reward.
- The dog may want to investigate the other pod before making the decision to indicate. As there is nothing in the other pod, it is unlikely to hold his interest and he will probably return to the food pod and indicate. However, if he indicates at the incorrect pod, lift it, and let him see there is nothing there. *Do not* put the pod back down on the floor – it needs to be eliminated from the decision-making process to ensure success. If the dog gives an incorrect indication several times in the same trial, it is a sign that you need to drop criteria as he is finding it too difficult at this stage. You will need to go back a few steps to establish learning before increasing the challenge.
- When your dog is taking up his passive indicator position on the food pod, over several trials, swap the pods so the food pod is second in line. Now the dog has to sniff the first pod, realise there is no scent, and move on to the second pod, where he will indicate, i.e., sit, as soon as he detects the smell of food. Repeat this for a few trials.
- Test your dog by randomly swapping the pods so sometimes the food pod is first in line, and sometimes second in line.
- Now add another pod, making three in total, and move the food pod around in the line, so it could be in position one, two or three. The dog must adopt his passive indicator position, i.e., go into a 'sit', at the food pod, without touching or playing with the pods or trying to get at the contents. As soon as he gives a positive indication – going into a 'sit' at the pod that contains food – lift the pod and hold on to it while you allow him to eat the treat.

FIND THE TOY
Objective: This short-term memory games involves the dog watching while his toy is hidden, performing a few easy tasks, and then remembering where it is.
What you need: A toy and two hiding places (under, or in something).

75

Canine Cognitive Skills

Allow the dog to watch as you hide the toy. Initially, make it easy by leaving part of the toy visible.

Now ask the dog to "find it".

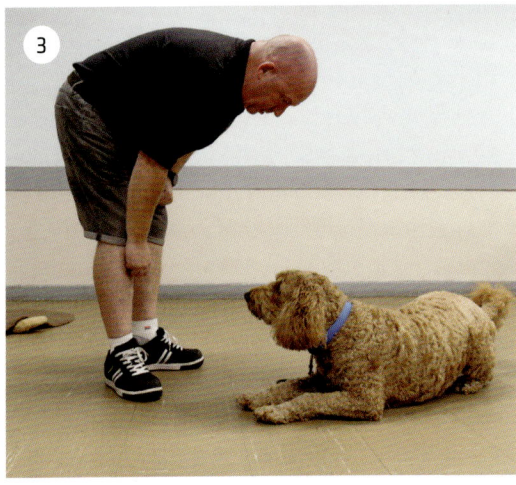

Progress to asking for a simple behaviour, such as a 'down' before sending him to find the toy.

Verbal cues:-
'Wait' – to wait on his base.
'Watch' – to observe the set-up of the exercise.
'Find it' – to send the dog to find his toy.
'Fetch' – to retrieve the toy.

We first need to find something that the dog will not mind having in his mouth, so the texture of the item you choose is important. You can use a favourite toy or, alternatively, can use an old flannel and tie it in a knot. This is easy to hold, and the dog's reward can be a game of tuggy. Ideally, the reward should involve the item the dog has found – tugging with it or playing chase with it – but this is not essential. In essence, the reward should be anything the dog values and will motivate him to play the game. In the following instructions, I will refer to a toy, and we will assume the dog enjoys playing tuggy. To play this game, the dog will need a solid retrieve (see *page 64*).

Step-by-step

- To start, make a toy 'special' by talking to it, caressing it and generally fussing over it. This will get your dog's attention and he will want to know what you have that is so valuable.
- Once you can see that he is interested, deny him sight of, or access to, the toy. Turn away from him and keep fussing the toy. When he follows you to see what it is, speak to him and ask him if he wants the toy. I have no doubt the answer will be 'yes!' Allow him to take hold of the toy and play a game of tuggy with him.
- Now take possession of the toy and ask your dog to go to his base and sit. Give him a chance to settle, and then – with a great show of excitement – invite him to play another short game of tuggy before taking possession again.
- Send the dog to his base and ask him to

"wait" and then "watch" as you hide the toy (hiding place A), with a little bit of it protruding so that the dog can see it.
- Return to your dog and ask him to "find it", but don't give him any further help. When he finds the toy and brings it to you, make a fuss of him and play a game of tuggy. You can use a verbal cue – 'fetch' – to tell him to bring the toy to you, but this may be unnecessary if 'find it' also means 'bring it to me'. Repeat this step several times, making sure the dog sees where you hide the toy so that that he is able to remember where it is.
- Now hide the toy in the same place (hiding place A), but this time it should be completely concealed, with no part sticking out. Return to the dog and ask him to "find it", and reward with a game of tuggy. Repeat several times.
- The next step is to ask for a simple behaviour before sending the dog to find the toy. It is important to make this as easy as possible so the dog knows exactly what to do. So, this time, let the dog watch you hide the toy (hiding place A), return to him and ask for a simple behaviour, such as "sit". Mark and reward with a treat, and then send him to find the toy. When he brings it back to you he gets a second reward – a game of tuggy. Repeat several times.

TRAINING TIP

If the dog fails to find the hidden toy, it indicates that he does not fully understand what he is required to do. If this is the case, drop the criteria by going back a step or two, and build from there.

- Now ask for two simple behaviours before sending him to find the toy. For example, this could be a 'sit' followed by a 'down'. It does not matter what you ask for as long as they are familiar behaviours that the dog performs, on cue, on a regular basis. Repeat several times, and don't forget to reward the dog with a game of tuggy so that he is learning to find the prize and then play with it.
- Step up the challenge and ask for three simple behaviours – for example, sit', 'down', 'stand' – before you send him to find the toy. Repeat several times.
- Now repeat all of the above steps, but use a different hiding place (hiding place B). You will need to work through each of the steps so the dog learns the whereabouts of the hiding place and remembers to go to it after performing a series of easy behaviours.
- Now that you have successfully used hiding places A and B, you can alternate between them, still asking for the three simple behaviours before sending the dog to find his toy. Can he perform these simple tasks and still remember where the toy is hidden?
- Over time, you may wish to increase criteria and add duration. Can the dog remember where the toy is hidden if you make him wait before sending him to find it? You could also increase the number of simple tasks you ask him to perform before sending him to find his toy. Or you could add another hiding place. Remember, the dog must be proficient at all previous steps before increasing the challenge.

MUFFIN MAN – Take One

Objective: The dog has to pick up tennis balls, which have been placed on a cake tray, to reveal hidden treats.

What you need: Treats, a cake tray, (I recommend a tray designed for muffins, as the balls stay in place and there is sufficient depth for the dog to pick up each ball cleanly), six tennis balls.

Canine Cognitive Skills

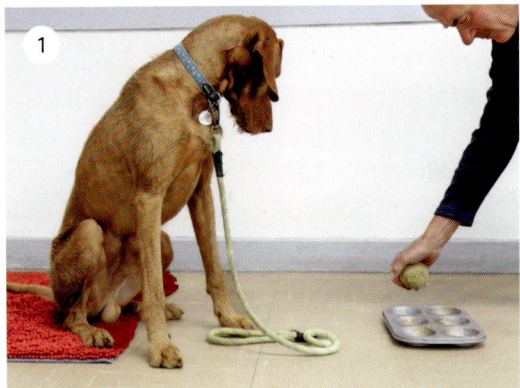

Allow the dog to watch as you place a treat in the muffin tray and then place a tennis ball on top of it.

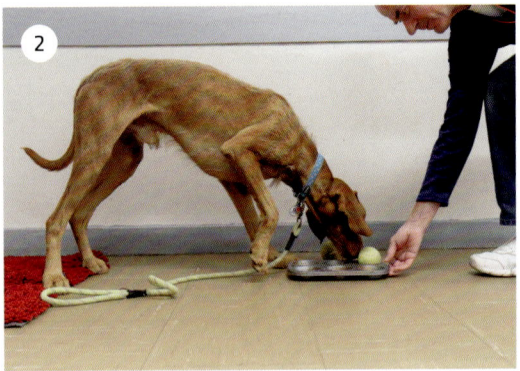

Now ask him to "find it".

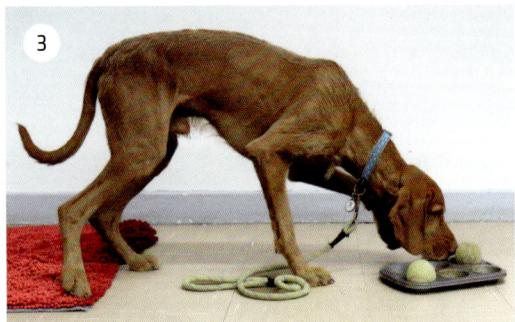

Gradually increase the number of balls and hidden treats.

Note: A small dog will find a standard tennis ball too big for his mouth, in which case you will need to source a smaller size. If you have a dog who does not like picking up and holding a tennis ball, you can use a rolled-up sock, or a small toy instead.

Verbal cues:-
'Wait' – to stay in position on his base.
'Watch' – to observe the set-up of the exercise.
'Find it' – to go and find the hidden treat.

Step-by-step
- Start with the dog on his base/anchor position and ask him to "wait" and 'watch' as you put a treat into the muffin tray and place a ball on top of it. Start with one ball.
- Encourage the dog to get the treat by himself, using his verbal cue "find it"; you could also gesture with your hand to indicate the muffin tray. At this stage, it does not matter whether he uses his nose, or a paw because he will soon realise (when you start using more balls) that it is quicker and easier to use his mouth to pick up the ball and get to the treat.
- Gradually increase the number of balls, plus hidden treats, making sure that the dog watches as you place treats in each compartment and then cover them with the tennis balls. Do not fall into the trap of nagging the dog, constantly repeating his "find it" cue. Remember, he needs that all important thinking time, so say the cue once, and let him work out what he has to do.
- Once the dog has grasped the exercise and has the confidence/motivation to continue playing, stay silent and leave him to work without verbal interference until it is time to mark and reward. If the dog needs some support, you could add "good" at occasional intervals so he keeps trying. If he is showing signs of insecurity and requires your verbal assistance for encouragement, it is ok to verbally mark each successful attempt.

INCREASING THE CHALLENGE

In this game the dog has to pick up the ball and place it in the muffin tray. Here, the dog is learning to play the game with a favourite toy.

MUFFIN MAN – Take Two

Objective: The dog has to pick up each tennis ball in turn, and place it *in* the cake tray.

What you need: Treats, muffin tray, six tennis balls (see Muffin Man – Take One for detailed information).

Verbal cues:-'
'Wait' – to stay in position for the set-up.
'Watch' – to observe the set-up for the exercise.
'Fetch' – to retrieve the ball.
'Ball in' – to drop the ball into the cake tray.

Step-by-step

- Start by sitting on the floor with the empty muffin tray in front of you, and the dog in front of the tray, so it should be: *you, tray, dog*.

- Pick up a tennis ball place it in front of the muffin tray, so it should be: *you, ball, tray, dog*. Now encourage the dog to pick up the ball. If you have trained a retrieve, you can use your 'fetch' cue. However, if the picking up and fetching concept is new to your dog, I suggest rolling the ball over a short distance, and then encouraging him to fetch it. If you are using a toy or a rolled-up sock in place of a tennis ball (see *page 78*), you can throw the item a short distance or simply drop it in front of your dog. The shorter the distance, the easier it will be for the dog to retrieve it and then complete the task. If he has to go to the other side of the room to retrieve it, he could get distracted and he is also out of position, which means you will need to encourage him to return to the vicinity of the tray.

- When the dog goes to pick up the ball, hold your open hands over the tray as if you are asking him to give you the ball, but do not attempt to take it, or to move your hands towards him as he approaches the tray. Your hands, hovering over the tray, are showing him that he must aim for this area.

- As he drops the ball into your hands, allow it to roll off and on to the tray. As it hits the tray, mark and reward by placing a treat in one of the empty compartments of the muffin tray. Repeat, even if the ball did not land or stay in a compartment. At this stage, the aim is to get the ball to land on the tray. It is important to reward from the tray, i.e., placing a treat in a compartment, so the dog learns that reinforcement only happens in the tray and, thus, he will be motivated to bring the ball as close to the tray as possible.

- With practice, the dog will learn that he must drop the ball into the empty compartment to earn his reward. When he is proficient, you can increase the challenge by asking him to drop additional balls into the tray until he is able to get all six tennis balls in place.

Chapter Seven
MASTER CLASS

To participate in a master class, a dog needs to have completed foundation work, and be proficient in a number of games outlined in the previous chapters, with a good understanding of the cues that are involved. This means he can focus on the task in hand, developing his existing learning as new challenges are presented.

BASIC SET-UP
As before, you will need basic set-up equipment, which includes:
- A bed/crate/platform to use as your dog's base.
- A pre-stuffed kong.
- Cut up treats.
- Fresh drinking water for your dog.

ADDITIONAL EQUIPMENT
Additional equipment will be referenced in the step-by-step instructions for each game. It includes:
- Coloured plates.
- Two identical containers, plus a third container of a different colour.
- Masking tape/Blu tac.
- Six scent pods (see *page 72*).
- Two prints with one spot, two prints with two spots, two prints with three spots.
- Coloured tubs.
- Two prints depicting picture pairs, two prints depicting shape pairs.
- Rags for toys.
- Tea towels.
- Three paper cups.
- Stool/chair/box.
- Red cups.
- Two pairs of blue/yellow items.
- Four prints depicting an ace, two prints depicting playing cards.

KEEPING WATCH
Objective: The dog has to keep track of a food cup (concealing a treat) when it is swapped between two empty cups.
What you need: Treats, three paper cups, all exactly the same shape and colour, a chair/stool/box.
Verbal cues:-
'Watch' – while you set up the exercise.
'Find it' – the dog is sent to find the cup with the treat.
'Wait" – given just before the dog reaches the cups.

Step-by-step
- Ask your dog to sit on his base/anchor position, and place a chair, a stool, or a box in front of him.

The surface area of the item needs to be level with the dog's head and with sufficient space to accommodate the three cups. This is because you want the dog to lean towards the cups rather than using his paws. In the following instructions, I will refer to a chair.

- Make sure your dog is watching you, then place a treat on the chair and immediately cover it with a cup. In all future trials, follow the procedure of placing the treat on the chair and then covering it with a cup, so your dog can see what you are doing. From now on, this will be the designated 'treat cup' as it will have the odour of food. It could be argued that he will learn that the cup with the treat has a stronger scent, but it will certainly make it easier if only one cup (the correct cup) smells of food.

MASTER CLASS

Allow the dog to watch as you place a treat under a cup – this will now be the designated treat cup, as it will smell of food. In the initial stages, it is easier for the dog if you place the cups on a chair, which will encourage him to lean towards them rather than trying to knock them over.

Once he understands he must keep watching the treat cup, you can work on swapping positions.

The dog gives a passive indication – a 'down' to show he has found the treat cup.

- Now ask the dog to "find it". The moment he stretches his neck towards the cup, mark and reward with the treat that has been secreted under the cup. Make sure you pick up the treat and give it to him, rather than letting him lean further forward, which would reinforce the behaviour of touching

KEEP IT CLEAN!

Try not to contaminate the other cups with the odour of treats from your hands. The best way to avoid this is to use one hand to touch food and the food cup, and the other hand to touch the two non-food cups. Although it is a bit tricky, you need to become adept at doing this so as to help the dog carry out the task.

the cup and maybe helping himself. Remember, the aim of the game is for the dog to indicate a stretch towards the cup (the correct cup) – not to actually touch it.

TRAINING TIP

If your dog touches the cup, be sure to mark him before he reaches it next time, when he is further away. You can then gradually start to mark him as he gets closer but is not within touching distance. I like to cue 'wait' at this point, as most dogs learn that 'wait' also means listen. The dog will, therefore, stop what he is doing – in this case going further towards the cup. This gives you the opportunity to mark, lift the cup and give the treat to the dog.

*In this way he will learn not to touch the cup, but simply go towards it. He will then freeze in position, and wait for you to mark and reward, i.e., the dog is always marked for **not** touching the cup so he learns not to. Timing is of the essence; if you mark when the dog touches the cup, and then reward him, this will be his (incorrect) goal going forward. The behaviour we want is for the dog to lean in towards the cup, thereby indicating where the treat is hidden.*

- Do not allow the dog to play with the cup or assume that he must knock it over. The trick is to indicate passively (without touching), towards the cup, but leave the cup in place.

If your dog knocks over the cup, say nothing. Re-start the game and, this time, make sure you mark him before he gets too close to the cup to touch it.

The next step is for the dog to maintain his focus on the food/treat cup as you move it. He needs to keep track of it, so that he can earn his reward:

- Place a treat on the chair and cover with the food cup. This will get and keep his attention on the cup for the next step.
- Picking up the cup up to move it will allow the dog to see the treat so make sure you *slide* it a few centimetres and then move it back to its original position. Ask the dog to "find it" and mark him as he leans forward to indicate, making sure he does not touch the cup. Repeat a few times. Moving the cup, and then returning it to its original position, teaches the dog to keep a close watch on the cup and note its position.
- Now place an empty cup alongside the food cup. At this stage we are *not* moving the empty cup; it is serving as a distraction. It will also help the dog to discriminate the 'non' rewarding cup (the empty one), thereby concentrating and following the rewarding treat cup.
- Next, place a treat on the chair and cover with the food cup. The order is important – place empty cup first, followed by food cup – as the dog will find it easier to recall the last item you touched. Allow the dog to watch as you slide the food cup to a difference position.
- Now focus on the food cup, and slide it a few centimetres in a direct line away from the empty cup, and then return it to its original position. Mark and reward the dog for a correct indication, i.e., the food cup. We want the dog to watch the cup with the treat under it and *not* to look at the empty cup (we will be adding another empty cup in due course, for more discrimination). The act of moving the food cup – and not the empty cup – means we are creating a history of paying attention exclusively to the food cup, so the dog learns that this is the reinforcing cup, not the empty one. Repeat a few times to create a history of this behaviour happening the same way each time.
- The next step is to move the empty cup first. Move it in a backwards direction, away from the dog, and then leave it where it is. The empty cup is now positioned further away from the dog, which will help him *not* to choose it. Now move the food cup in a straight line, either left or right, but not backwards and then return it to its original place. Ask the dog to "find it" and when he gives a correct indication, mark and reward as before. Keep working on this to establish learning. If he makes a mistake, say nothing. Start again and if mistakes keep happening, drop criteria to help the dog get it right.
- Place the empty cup first. Follow this by placing the treat and covering it with the food cup. Then move the food cup in a forward direction towards the dog and ask him to "find it" in its new position. Mark and reward.
- It is now time to add a second empty cup. Place both empty cups first, followed by a treat, which is then covered with the food cup. Ask the dog to "find it. Mark and reward for a correct indication.
- Follow the same procedure, placing the empty cups, followed by the treat and then cover it with the food cup, but now move the food cup to different positions – sometimes closer to the dog, sometimes on the far side of the empty cups – but never behind an empty cup. Our goal is to play the game with all three cups in a row, so

MASTER CLASS

work towards this gradually. Remember, you are only moving the food cup, which encourages the dog to watch it intently and ignore the other two.
- Keep working on this to establish a strong behaviour of focusing on the food cup and ignoring the others so that he is able to identify it no matter how many times it has swapped postion.
- If the dog is proficient, you can increase the challenge and try moving the empty cups as well.

WATCH, SMELL, REMEMBER!

Objective: A memory and scent test, challenging the dog to indicate the scent pod with a treat hidden underneath it.

What you need: Treats, scent pods (starting with one and building up to a maximum of four at the end of the exercise). You can also use football cones or takeaway boxes (see *page 72*).

Verbal cues:-
'Wait' – while you set up the exercise.
'Watch' – to observe what you are doing.
'Find it' – to ask the dog to identify the pod.

This is a game of scent detection. The dog has to find the food pod, no matter where it is positioned in the line-up.

To start the task, use your verbal cue "find it".

The set-up.

Success!

Step-by-step

- Ask your dog to go to his base/anchor position so that he can watch you set up the exercise. Initially, we will start with one pod, as we need to teach the dog not to play with it, but to offer a passive indicator (a sit or a down, depending on what you have taught him). This draws on the learning established in Keeping watch (see *page 80*).
- When your dog is confidently offering a passive indicator on the food pod, you are ready to introduce more pods – one at a time – but don't incorporate the food pod at this stage. Make it easy for the dog by arranging the pods in a straight line so that he can travel from one pod to the next without needing to double back. There should be a reasonable distance between the pods.
- Now place a treat within the pattern, and cover it with the food pod. As with Keeping watch (see *page 80*), it is important to have a designated food pod and ensure that the other pods you use are not contaminated with the smell of food.
- Ask the dog to "find it", using your arm in a sweeping movement, to indicate the pods. In fact, this may be superfluous as the dog has watched you set up the game from his base. He will also have seen you placing the treat but, in all likelihood, he will go straight to the nearest pod to start his search.
- When he has found the correct pod and signalled his find with a sit or a down (passive indicator), mark and reward him, using the treat under the food pod.
- Send the dog to back to his base and pick up all the pods. Set out the pods in a different pattern and, this time, introduce a memory test by positioning the food pod second to last, i.e., place the food pod, followed by your last pod. When you ask your dog to "find it" he will, most likely, go to the last pod you put down. However, when he fails to find a food scent, he will continue to search. The aim of the game is for the dog to watch you place the pod, to use his sense of smell to find the food pod, and to remember which pods he has already searched.

TRAINING TIP

When your dog is searching, keep quiet. Do not keep repeating his verbal cue. We don't need to keep asking him when he is already doing it!

- To progress the game, you create different patterns with the pods – for example, a triangle or a diamond – so your dog has to be systematic in searching all the pods. You can also place the food pod earlier on in the set-up, making it the first or second pod you place in order to increase the memory challenge.

TALKING PICTURES

Objective: The dog learns to respond to a verbal cue to find the correct visual image.
What you need: Treats, two different pictures, for example, a pig and a tree, (preferably laminated), food bowl, masking tape/Blu Tac.
Verbal cues:-
'Watch' – to observe the set-up of the exercise.
 'Show me' – to indicate his choice.
   A one-word cue to name the image, e.g. 'tree', 'pig' (examples I will use in the following instructions).
   In this game, the dog uses a process of visual discrimination and informed choice to identify the image you are cueing by name. The images should be silhouettes or

MASTER CLASS

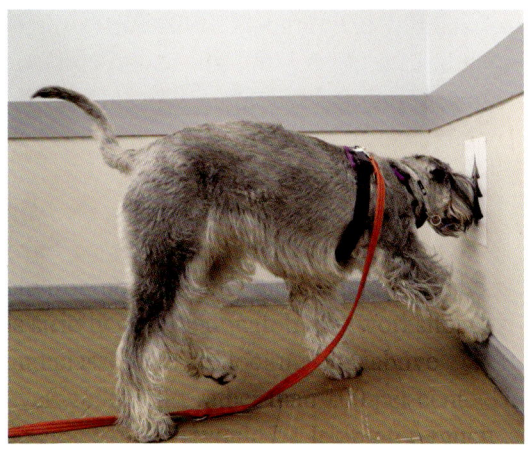

When the dog has learnt to target the image, you can name it – in this case "tree". He will then learn to distinguish this print from any other non-rewarding print.

line drawings – nothing too fussy or too complicated – to make it as easy as possible for the dog.

Step-by-step

- Station your dog on his base and ask him to "watch". Choose which image you are going to start with and attach it to the wall in the area in which you will be working your dog. I will start with the picture of a tree. Set up the food bowl behind the dog's start position. Don't stand too far away from the wall – a metre will suffice.
- Ask the dog to target the tree picture, using an outstretched arm, and the verbal cue, 'show me'. At this point, we are not naming the image, just getting the dog to target it. Mark and reward by tossing a treat in the food bowl behind the dog. This will encourage him to turn directly towards you ready for the next rep. Repeat a couple of times.
- Now repeat the previous step, but this time, introduce the verbal cue 'tree', as you indicate the image with your outstretched arm. The dog will go to the wall and target the tree because it is the only available choice. However, in the process he will start to commit the picture of the tree to memory. Mark and reward as before.
- Now add a non-rewarding picture on the wall, e.g., an image of a pig, so the dog has to discriminate and target the picture that will yield a reward. Help him by standing on the side of the picture that you want him to target, just as you did with previous games (see *page 70*).
- Now swap sides and continue to give the verbal cue for the image you want the dog to target, e.g., "tree", before sending him to the wall. If he makes an incorrect choice, do nothing. This will encourage him to try the other option and get a reward.
- Once your dog can verbally and visually identify two images, and is achieving an above average success rate of six out of 10, regardless of where you stand, you can add a third image, e.g. a picture of a flower. Work on this over a series of reps, before you attempt to add more images.

COUNT THE SPOTS

Objective: To look at a sample print and indicate the print with the corresponding number of spots. In reality, the dog is not counting the spots, but he is committing the patterns to memory and responding to a verbal cue.

What you need: Treats, two A4 prints with one spot, two A4 prints with two spots, two A4 prints with three spots, plus a blank A4 print, masking tape/Blu Tac.

Verbal cues:-

'One', 'Two', 'Three' – naming the number of spots.
'Look' – to focus on the prints.
'Show me' – to indicate his choice.

Canine Cognitive Skills

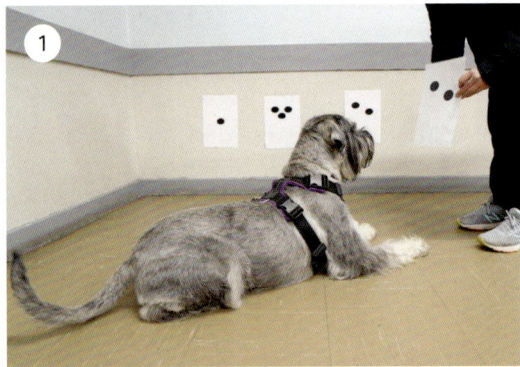

In order to 'count the spots', the dog memorises the pattern.

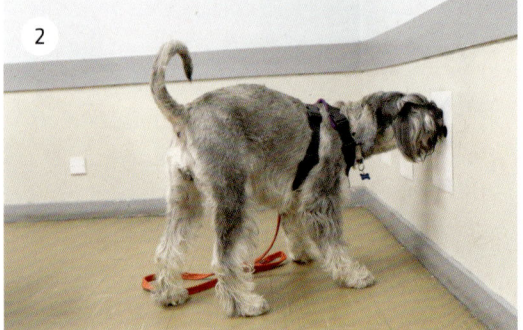

He then matches it with the corresponding print on the wall.

Step-by-step

- Start by attaching a print with one spot on the wall and ask your dog to touch. As he nose-touches the print, say "one", and throw a treat behind the dog – away from the wall – so he is ready to reset for the next trial after eating his treat.
- Place the corresponding one-spot print on the floor in front of you. Bring your hands downwards to the print and give the verbal cue, " look". Then point to the print with one dot on the wall and say "show me". When your dog touches the print on the wall, mark and reward. Repeat several times.
- Now place a blank print on the wall next to the one-spot print. This is similar to noughts and crosses (see *page 67*), where we use a blank non-rewarding print for discrimination purposes. If the dog nose touches the blank print, say and do nothing. Simply wait and see if the dog opts for the one-spot print in order to earn his reward. He will soon work out where the reinforcement lies and offer the correct behaviour.
- Next, attach a two-spot print to the wall but continue to ask for "one", marking and rewarding the correct choice. The dog has to discriminate between the prints because, at the moment, only the one-spot print is paying dividends.
- Remove the one-spot print from the wall, leaving the blank and the two-spot print in place. Now place the second two-spot print on the floor and ask the dog to "look" and then "show me" to indicate his choice. Mark and reward each successful trial.
- Re-attach the one-spot print to the wall and continue to cue "look".
- Now remove the two-spot print and the blank print from the wall. Leave the one-spot print in place, and attach a three-spot print to the wall, with a corresponding sample print, face up, on the floor. Ask the dog to "look" and then ask him to go to the wall and indicate his choice, "show me".

Note: The sample print – in this case, the three-spot print – is always face up on the floor so the dog can identify it before making his choice, i. e., see, then choose. In time, the 'look' cue can be replaced by naming the print, 'one', 'two', 'three', but wait until learning is fully established and the dog is achieving a high success rate. This takes time, so be patient.

- Add the blank print to the wall and continue clicking and rewarding the dog for touching the three-spot print.
- Finally, remove the blank print and add the one-spot print.

COLOUR DISCRIMINATION

Objective: The dog learns which coloured pot contains high value treats.

What you need: Treats (high value, e.g. chicken or anything else you know is high value to your dog, and low value, e.g. carrot, apple, kibble, etc), two coloured pots or bowls. Dogs finds it easiest to see blue and yellow so you may choose to use these colours in the initial stages of training. The pots can be any type of container, the only stipulation is that they need to be big enough so the dog can eat from them.

Verbal cues:-
'Watch' – to observe the set-up of the exercise.
'Find it' – to go and investigate the pots.
'Sit'/'Down' – passive indicator position offered freely by the dog. Training for this needs to be established before attempting to play this game (see Show and tell, *page 72*).
'Take it' – permission to eat the treat.

This is a game of learned choice, where the dog learns that one pot of a particular colour (e.g., green) contains the high value treat, and the other differently coloured pot (e.g., pink) contains a less favourable treat. It is not entirely dependent on scent; the dog has to work out where to find the good stuff by identifying the correct colour (green) and, discriminating against the other colour (pink).

It does not matter which colour you choose for the high value treats, but it must *always* be the same one. In the following instructions I will use the green pot for high value treats.

After visiting the pots and eating the treats, the dog will learn to favour the cup containing his most desired treat. He will visit it first, followed by the other pot where he might eat the less favourable treat or leave it *in situ*. It may be that the dog does not choose to visit the lesser value treat pot at all, or you may have a greedy dog who will take his chances to eat them both in any order! Ultimately colour recognition, scent and applied learning come into play, but during the learning process, you will see how your dog is improving his skill set to be not only more successful, but also quicker to reach his high value reward.

The dog watches the treat being placed in the green pot. This is the high value pot.

When he is asked to "find it", he will be rewarded by finding the high value treat in the green pot.

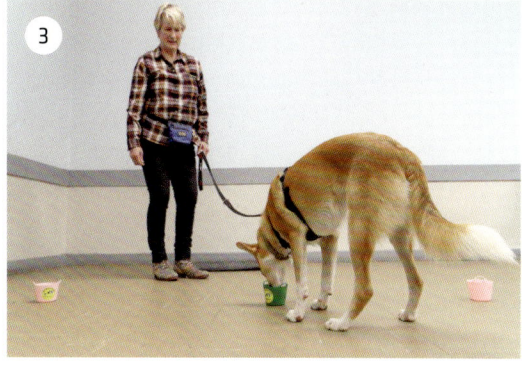

In time, he will learn that the green pot always contains the high value treat – no matter where it is placed in line-up – and he will ignore the pink pots. You can then progress to asking for a passive indicator – a 'sit' or a 'down' – when he identifies the green pot.

Canine Cognitive Skills

Step-by-step

- Start by asking your dog to go to his base/anchor position so he can watch you place the two pots – one green pot and one pink pot – in a horizonal line in front of him, approximately 1m apart. Now put a high value treat in the green pot, and a low value treat in the pink pot. It does not matter whether you start with the high value treat on the dog's left or right but remember, the high value treat must always go in the same-coloured pot, in this instance, the green pot.
- Now ask your dog to investigate – "find it" – and observe as he makes his choice. At this stage, we are not asking for a passive indicator, i.e., a sit or a down, as he reaches the high value pot. Allow the dog to approach the pots and eat his choice of treats. Do this a few times to create learning history, i.e., good treats in the green pot, not so good in the pink pot.
- Then, after a few trials, as the dog approaches the green pot (high value), ask for your passive indicator *before* he gets there. Once he has offered the position quickly join him and give him a cue 'take it', allowing him to consume his reward.
- Swap the pots so that sometimes the high value cup is on the left and sometimes it is on the right. You can then increase the challenge by adding more pots to the line up.

What an effective way to test which treats your dog prefers!

COLOUR MATCH

Objective: Learning the colour of an item, and matching it to a corresponding item of the same colour.

What you need: Treats, pairs of matching items – for example, two blue gloves (or you can use cut-outs of hands), two yellow socks, two blue cup coasters, two yellow ducks. Stick to using blue and yellow as dogs find these colours easiest to identify.

Note: It is not important what the item is, but they need to be identical. One is a sample to show the dog, the other will be used as the target.

Verbal cues:-

'Look' – to focus on the coloured item.
'Show me' – to indicate his choice.

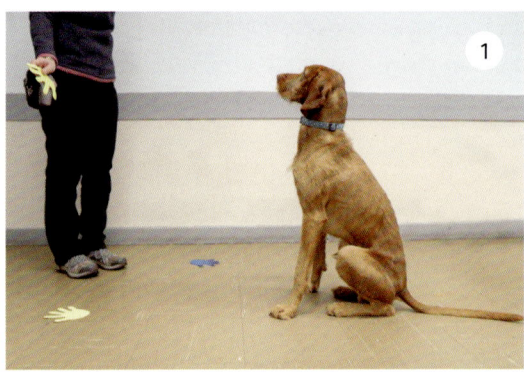

The set-up.

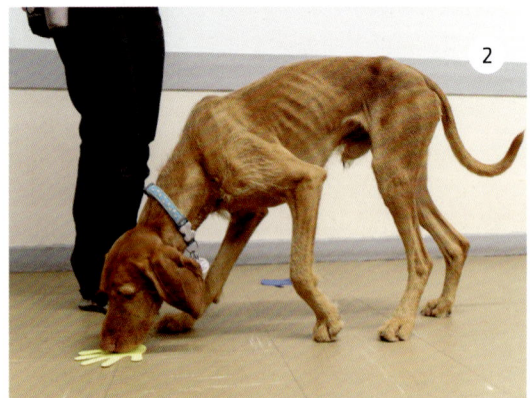

The dog indicates the matching-coloured item.

Step-by-step

- Select a pair of coloured items (in the following instructions I will use blue gloves). Ask the dog to sit on his bed, which should be positioned a short distance from you. He needs to be able to watch

what you are doing but not approach until he is cued.
- Place one of the blue gloves on the floor to your left or right. It does not matter which side, but for these instructions we will use the left side. Hold the other glove in your left hand and then put your left hand behind your back.
- Say the dog's name to get his attention.
- Show him the blue glove in your left hand, producing it from behind your back, and giving the verbal cue, 'look'. When you are confident that the dog has focused on the glove in your hand, put it back behind your back.
- Now give the verbal cue, 'show me' and look at the other blue glove which is located on the floor to your left. As there is only one item available, the dog will immediately go to the glove on the floor. This is correct so you can mark and reward.

TRAINING TIP
The reinforcement needs to be delivered as quickly as possible to mark the correct behaviour, so it helps if you wear a treat bag or position a bowl of treats close by.

- Repeat several times making sure the dog is looking at the blue glove in your hand first and then targeting the glove on the floor. There is only one option available so the dog is building up a history of correct behaviour and reinforcement, which means he will repeat the behaviour.
- Now put the blue glove in your *right* hand, and hold it behind your back. Leave the other glove on the floor, on your left, as before.
- Show the dog the glove in your right hand, saying "look". and then put it behind your back. Now say "show me" to indicate the blue glove on the floor. Although there is only one choice, you have changed the position of the glove on the floor. The dog is learning to target the blue glove regardless of where it is located. Once he has done this successfully a few times, you can move the glove to different positions on the floor to cement his learning.
- Now the fun starts! This is the point where you place a differently-coloured item on the floor, which is purely for discrimination purposes. The set-up remains the same as before but, in addition, place a yellow glove on the floor to your right. Now, when you show the dog the blue glove in your hand, he needs to ignore the yellow glove on the floor and target the blue glove. Make this exercise as easy as possible, positioning the gloves on the floor at a distance from each other, and also ensuring the dog is focusing on the glove in your hand before you give your 'show me' cue. Mark and reward as soon as he targets the blue glove. Repeat several times.

TRAINING TIP
You can help your dog by looking at the blue glove on the floor and ignoring the yellow glove, as he may look at you for direction. At this stage, you want the learning to be error-free so the dog is successful – and is reinforced – every time. You can increase the challenge later on when he fully understands the concept of the game.

Once the dog is successful at this stage, you can raise criteria by introducing a yellow glove from behind your back as follows:
- Position a blue glove on the floor to your left and a yellow glove to your right. Hold the other yellow glove in your right hand,

Canine Cognitive Skills

behind your back. Show it to the dog and ask him to "look" and then put it back behind your back. Now say "show me" and look at the yellow glove on the floor which should help him to target it. Make sure you mark him instantly for making the correct choice and reward. Repeat this step several times.

- When you think your dog is ready, you can alternate between blue and yellow trials, or mix it up by doing two blue trials followed by one yellow trial. In this way the dog learns he needs to look at the sample and then match it with the item of the same colour on the floor. At this stage, it important to keep the blue glove on your left, and the yellow glove on your right.

- The next step is to produce the sample blue glove in your left hand, and position the corresponding blue glove on your *right* side. The yellow glove is presented in your right hand, but the yellow glove on the floor is positioned on your *left* side. You may not think this looks very different but the dog has become accustomed to seeing the blue glove on your left side (his right) and the yellow glove on your right side (his left). He now has to match the sample, regardless of whether it is on your left or on your right. Repeat several times.

- If your dog is successful you can try swapping between your left and your right hand when you are presenting the blue and yellow gloves. To make it easier, do not change the position of the gloves on the floor for a few trials.

- The final challenge is to present the samples from either your left or your right hand and ask the dog to indicate the corresponding item regardless of where it is positioned on the floor.

CHASE THE ACE

Objective: The dog has to pick out the ace from a number of different playing cards.
What you need: Treats, Four A4 prints depicting an ace, two prints depicting other playing cards – all printed in black and white.
Verbal cues:-
'Watch' – to observe the set-up
'Find it' or 'Chase the ace' – to go and find the ace.

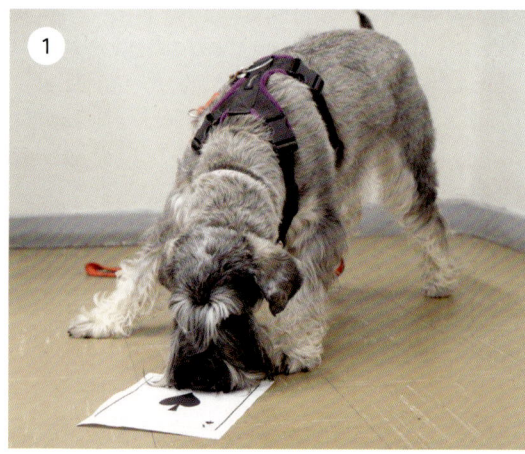

Start by making the ace highly rewarding.

With practice, the dog will learn to pick out the high-value ace from a number of non-rewarding cards.

Step-by-step

- Start by making the ace print highly rewarding to the dog. Stand in front of him, holding the print, and ask him to "find it". As you are standing, he is likely to offer a nose touch. Reward every indication.
- Keep repeating until the dog indicates the

ace print without a verbal cue. This is to test whether he will offer the behaviour without being prompted. Stay still and silent and wait for the dog to indicate. This will only happen if you have already asked him to perform the behaviour and reinforced accordingly.

- Now place the ace print on the floor in front of you, ask the dog to "find it"/"chase the ace" and wait for him to target with a nose touch, or a paw if your dog has a history of choosing a paw touch as a preference. When the dog indicates, mark and reward by tossing a treat away from the print so he can then choose to return and repeat the behaviour.
- Walk away from the ace print and then return to it. Wait for the dog to target the ace so you can, again, mark, and reward.
- Now place a second ace print on the floor and mark and reward the dog every time he indicates – it doesn't matter which one he chooses.
- You are now ready to place the other two ace prints on the floor (making a total of four). Walk around the prints with your dog and if he stops to indicate, mark and reward by placing a treat on top of the ace print he has chosen. Continue doing this until he has indicated all four aces. You can also reinforce if he indicates the same ace twice, as he is still offering the desired behaviour.
- Now place a print depicting a different playing card on the floor. This is for discrimination purposes only. The dog will not earn a reward if he indicates it, so walk past it, allowing background learning to take place (i.e., the dog learns to ignore it).
- Gradually add two or three non-rewarding cards but only reward when the dog indicates an ace. He will be quick to learn that it is the ace that has value – the other prints can be safely ignored. Initially make sure there are more aces than non-rewarding cards, and only increase the ratio when he fully understands the concept.

There are many variations of this game, all taught the same way, such as:
- Find the dog picture amongst other animals. (non-dog of course)
- Find the dog's name. Abbreviate the name to a maximum of four letters, as the dog will find it harder to learn if there are too many characters. If the name cannot be shortened, use a nickname.
- Find the dog's breed – among images of other breeds.

You will probably be able to think of some different ideas once your dog understands the concept.

PICTURE RECALL

Objective: The dog has to look at an image, memorise it, and then pick out a matching image, which is displayed on a wall.

What you need: Treats, sets of A4 prints containing two matching pictures. This could be two trees, two spoons, two cats, two mice, a blank A4 print, masking tape/Blu Tac.

Note: Ideally, the images should be depicted as black silhouettes against a white background. When the dog becomes a little more experienced, you could add more detail to the images – but still in black and white.

Verbal cues:-
'Sit' – starting position for the exercise.
'Wait' – to stay in position and listen to what comes next.
'Look' – to focus on the images.
'Show me' – to indicate his choice.

When your dog understands the concept, you can increase the challenge by naming the images you want him to target.

Canine Cognitive Skills

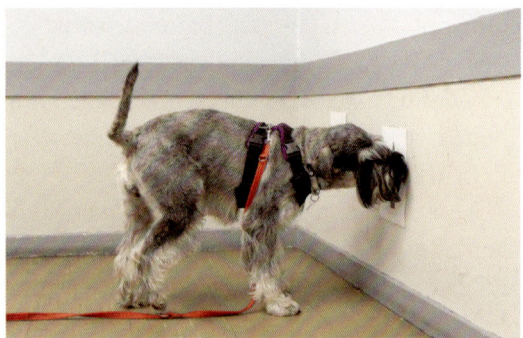

The dog has to memorise the image he is shown, and then indicate the matching print on the wall.

Step-by-step
- Attach a picture print on the wall. Starting with a single image makes it easier and helps the dog to understand the concept of the game. For the purpose of these instructions, I will start with the image of a tree.
- Place a matching tree print on the floor and cover it with a towel so the dog cannot see it. Ask the dog to sit and wait. Remove the towel and allow the dog to look at the picture for a few seconds. You can focus his attention by using your verbal cue, 'look', but, in all likelihood, he will look at the print as you have asked him to 'wait' which effectively means 'stay in position and listen to what comes next'. Removing the towel will also focus his attention.
- If he tries to target the print, use your hand signal and ask him to "wait". He should stop in his tracks. Now ask him to "sit" and "wait" again. If your dog has a good 'stay' cue, you could use 'sit' and 'stay' and then pick up the towel.
- Now cover the tree print again and ask the dog to "wait". Then, using a sweeping arm gesture towards the tree print on the wall, use your 'show me' cue to ask him to target the matching print. In most cases, this will be a nose touch. Mark and reward by tossing the treat away from the wall so the dog is ready for the next trial. Work on 10 reps and if the dog is achieving a high ratio of success, you are ready to raise criteria. If this is not the case, continue with this step a little longer until learning is established.
- When you think your dog is ready, attach a second picture print (for example, a cat) to the wall for discrimination purposes. The dog needs to continue targeting the tree print which matches the sample print on the floor.
- Now swap samples and place the cat print on the floor. Go through the same process as before:
  - Cover the print with a towel.
  - Remove the towel and ask the dog to "look" at the print.
  - Cover the print again.
  - Send him to target the corresponding print on the wall, using your 'show me' cue.
- When the dog clearly understands the concept of the game, add another picture print (for example, a spoon) to the wall, and introduce the corresponding sample print as before. Each time the dog identifies the correct picture, he is mentally taking in the other pictures so he will be ready to match them when you present the relevant print.

LIKE FOR LIKE
Objective: The dog has to pick out the matching item you have shown him (e.g. a red glove) from a couple of other items. This is similar to the colour match game (see *page 88*) but instead of restricting it to a solid-coloured item, you can now use multi-coloured items, as long as both items are identical.

What you need: Treats, three matching items (for example, two red gloves, two plastic bottle and two tennis balls); it doesn't really matter what you use as long as you have two of each item and they are identical.

Verbal cues:-

'Sit' – the starting position.

'Wait' – to stay in position, ignore all distractions and wait for the next instruction.

'Look' – to focus on the sample item.

'Show me' – to indicate his choice.

'Fetch' – to go and retrieve the item (advanced option).

There are three items to choose from, but the dog has to match the one he has been shown.

Step-by-step

- Ask the dog to sit on his bed/anchor position, a short distance away from you. He needs to be able to watch what you are doing, but stay in position until he is cued to come forward.
- To establish learning, start with one pair of items, such as a pair of red gloves. As with the colour match game (see *page 88*), place one of the red gloves on the floor to your left or right side. Here I will start on the left side. Hold the other red glove in your left hand, behind your back.
- Say the dog's name so that he is focusing on you, produce the red glove from behind your back and show it to the dog. Use your verbal cue, 'look'.
- Once the dog has looked at the glove in your hand, put it back behind your back and say: "show me' as you look at the glove on the floor. As there is only one item available, the dog will target the glove on the floor. He has shown the correct behaviour so you can mark and reward. Ideally, you will be wearing a treat bag, or you can position a bowl of treats nearby so you can be quick to reward. Repeat this step several times making sure the dog is looking at the red glove in your hand first and then targeting the glove on the floor. The repetition of correct behaviour – and reinforcement – means he is more likely to repeat the behaviour.
- Now hold the red glove in your *right* hand, behind your back. Leave the other red glove on the floor on your left as per the previous step. Show the dog the glove in your right hand, saying "look", put it back behind your back, and then say "show me" to indicate the glove on the floor.
- Although there is still only one choice, we have changed the position of the glove on the floor so the dog is learning to target the red glove, regardless of where it is. Once he has been successful a few times, you can move the glove to different positions on the floor. He now understands that targeting the glove – the only available option – is the route to reinforcement.
- You are now ready to introduce a new item – for example, a plastic bottle – but for discrimination purposes only! Everything remains the same – you simply place a plastic bottle on the floor to your right. Show the dog the sample red glove from behind your back, and give your verbal cue, 'show me'. The dog has to target the red glove on the floor and ignore the plastic bottle.

- If the dog goes to the plastic bottle – and he might, just to sniff it and check it out – say and do nothing. Wait. The dog will realise that nothing is happening and so he needs to do something different. He only has one option – the red glove – so he will be successful, allowing you to mark and reward. Keep repeating this step to build up a history of success.
- Once the dog understands what he has to do, you can produce the glove in your *right* hand but leave the other glove on your left side and the bottle on your right side, as before.
- Next, move the items on the floor, and present the sample in either your left or your right hand.

TRAINING TIP

Take your time! If you rush through these initial steps, the dog does not have the opportunity to learn through trial and error. This learning is essential as it allows him to progress by making informed choices, thereby increasing his success rate until errors are few and far between.

- When the dog has built up a good success ratio, you can produce the plastic bottle from behind your back. Ask him to "look" and then "show me", directing your gaze at the plastic bottle on the floor. Be quick to mark and reward a correct choice. Although this is the first time you have produced the plastic bottle from behind your back, the dog is already familiar with it because he has been discriminating against it when he has selected the red glove. This type of background learning is very useful!
- If the dog does go to an incorrect item, again say nothing and keep still. Do not look directly at the dog because otherwise he will just look back at you waiting for direction. Instead, look at the item on the floor that you want him to choose. This is the only clue you are going to give him. If you offer help, he will just learn to hold out for your assistance and will not engage his brain and have a go. Remember, just like us, dogs are keen to find the fastest route to reinforcement!
- Over time, you work with all three pairs of items – adding a pair of tennis balls, for example, remembering that the more items you use, the harder it is for the dog! Don't rush to add more items. Practise until your dog is perfect before increasing the number.

ADVANCED OPTIONS

After you have gone through all the above steps, and your dog can indicate each item after being shown the sample, you can increase the challenge:

- Move the items around on the floor in front of you so that there is no order to how they are laid out. This will really make him think!
- Now place the items further away from you. First ask the dog to "look" at the sample, then say "show me", followed by "fetch' so that he brings the item back to you. Depending on how you have taught a retrieve, the dog can either drop it in front of you or deliver to your hand. For the purposes of this game, the priority is choosing the correct item.

COGNITIVE LEARNING FROM THIS GAME
- Match and sample
- Learning new items
- Listening skills

IN CONCLUSION

Working your way through the games in this book, I hope that you and your dog have discovered some new and fun ways to keep your brains ticking over!

Remember to keep the games easy to start with, increasing the level of difficulty, bit by bit, when you can see your dog is ready for an increase in criteria.

Above all, keep the learning experience positive so your dog chooses to participate. Work at his pace, and keep the rewards coming so he has a handsome payback for his efforts.

Regardless of what stage you reach, your dog will be giving his brain a real workout as he improves visual and listening skills, learns how to discriminate, make decisions and problem solve. You are playing fun games together but, as his cognitive skills improve, you will notice that he will grow in confidence as you are giving him the most precious of all gifts – one that allows him to cope with everyday life with flexibility, with resilience, and with boundless enthusiasm!